SpringerBriefs in Economics

AF212607

More information about this series at http://www.springer.com/series/8876

Hirofumi Uchida · Arito Ono
Souichirou Kozuka · Makoto Hazama
Iichiro Uesugi

Interfirm Relationships and Trade Credit in Japan

Evidence from Micro-Data

Springer

Hirofumi Uchida
Graduate School of Business Administration
Kobe University
Kobe
Hyogo
Japan

Makoto Hazama
Graduate School of Economics
Hitotsubashi University
Kunitachi
Tokyo
Japan

Arito Ono
Research Department
Mizuho Research Institute
Chiyoda-ku
Tokyo
Japan

Iichiro Uesugi
Institute of Economic Research
Hitotsubashi University
Kunitachi
Tokyo
Japan

Souichirou Kozuka
Faculty of Law
Gakushuin University
Toshima-ku
Tokyo
Japan

ISSN 2191-5504 ISSN 2191-5512 (electronic)
ISBN 978-4-431-55186-7 ISBN 978-4-431-55187-4 (eBook)
DOI 10.1007/978-4-431-55187-4

Library of Congress Control Number: 2014946404

Springer Tokyo Heidelberg New York Dordrecht London

© The Author(s) 2015
This work is subject to copyright. All rights are reserved by the Publisher, whether the whole or part of the material is concerned, specifically the rights of translation, reprinting, reuse of illustrations, recitation, broadcasting, reproduction on microfilms or in any other physical way, and transmission or information storage and retrieval, electronic adaptation, computer software, or by similar or dissimilar methodology now known or hereafter developed. Exempted from this legal reservation are brief excerpts in connection with reviews or scholarly analysis or material supplied specifically for the purpose of being entered and executed on a computer system, for exclusive use by the purchaser of the work. Duplication of this publication or parts thereof is permitted only under the provisions of the Copyright Law of the Publisher's location, in its current version, and permission for use must always be obtained from Springer. Permissions for use may be obtained through RightsLink at the Copyright Clearance Center. Violations are liable to prosecution under the respective Copyright Law.
The use of general descriptive names, registered names, trademarks, service marks, etc. in this publication does not imply, even in the absence of a specific statement, that such names are exempt from the relevant protective laws and regulations and therefore free for general use.
While the advice and information in this book are believed to be true and accurate at the date of publication, neither the authors nor the editors nor the publisher can accept any legal responsibility for any errors or omissions that may be made. The publisher makes no warranty, express or implied, with respect to the material contained herein.

Printed on acid-free paper

Springer is part of Springer Science+Business Media (www.springer.com)

Preface

In this monograph, we describe the current status of firm interrelationships in Japan by using a unique and huge data set that covers about 380,000 firms. To grasp the entirety of this huge dataset, which is almost the same as a picture of all firms in current Japan, we summarize the descriptive statistics of the variables and conduct statistical analyses. Further, we put special emphasis on trade credit between firms. The payment for interfirm transactions is usually made on account, or by payment after the delivery, rather than by immediate payment. Therefore, late payment is nothing but a provision of credit from a seller to a buyer, and hence, interfirm lending/borrowing is called *trade credit*. Trade credit is used all over the world and accounts for a non-negligible portion of the firms' balance sheets. We provide comprehensive information on to what extent, and in what terms, firms in Japan transact through trade credit—to a level of detail that has not been available for other countries. The uniqueness of this monograph also lies in its description of the legal background in Japan. In any country, the legal structure prescribes the basis of corporate activities.

For those researchers who want to grasp economic activities in the real economy, one of the major challenges is the lack of data availability. As for the interfirm activities, researchers have encountered serious difficulties due to the lack of detailed data. In this monograph, we make use of data that enable us to describe the current status of interfirm relationships in Japan in great detail. This data was made possible through the cooperation with Teikoku Databank Ltd., one of the largest credit information providers in Japan. The main data are from their credit reports from 2007 to 2010 and from the accompanying financial statement data.

This monograph has a companion paper (Ono et al. forthcoming). This monograph focuses on interfirm relationships in Japan, but Ono et al. (forthcoming) focus on firm-bank relationships in Japan using the same dataset. Taking information from this paper and from the present monograph, we can grasp the whole picture of the current status of the relationships of Japanese firms with their trade partners as well as financial institutions.

Organization of this Brief

The remaining part of this monograph is composed as follows. In Sect. 1 we briefly describe the original TDB data and our sample selection process. Section 2 presents the descriptive statistics and obtains an image of our sample firms. We also discuss the representativeness of our sample and conduct some preliminary analysis in Sect. 2. Section 3 provides a detailed description and conducts some analysis on trade credit in Japan. In Sect. 4, we describe the legal framework in Japan. Section 5 concludes the monograph.

Acknowledgments

This monograph is based on a study of our project “Designing Industrial and Financial Networks to Achieve Sustainable Economic Growth” under the Ministry of Education, Culture, Sports, Science and Technology’s program “Promoting Social Science Research Aimed at Solutions of Near-Future Problems.” We gratefully thank the Ministry of Education, Culture, Sports, Science, and Technology for its financial support, Teikoku Databank Ltd. for providing data, and Masahiro Miyatani and Takurou Kitou for their technical support. We also acknowledge Gregory Udell, Jonathan Moore, Masaji Kano, Noriyuki Yanagawa, Daisuke Tsuruta, Koji Sakai, and Takashi Hatakeda for their helpful comments. The views expressed in this monograph are those of the authors and do not necessarily reflect those of the institutions with which they are affiliated.

Reference

Ono, A., H. Uchida, S. Kozuka, and M. Hazama. A new look at bank-firm relationships and the use of collateral in Japan: Evidence from Teikoku Databank Data. In The Economics of Interfirm Networks (Advances in Japanese Business and Economics, Volume 4), Chap. 12, eds. T. Watanabe, I. Uesugi, and A. Ono, Springer, forthcoming.

Contents

About the Authors

Makoto Hazama is a graduate student at Hitotsubashi University. He served as a research assistant in the project "Design of Inter-firm Networks to Achieve Sustainable Economic Growth" under the Program for Promoting Social Science Research Aimed at Solutions of Near-Future Problems, conducted by the Japan Society for the Promotion of Science (2009–2012). He is working as a research assistant for the Research Institute of Economy, Trade, and Industry.

Souichirou Kozuka is a professor at Gakushuin University, Tokyo. He holds a Ph.D. in law from Tokyo University and had taught at Chiba University and Sophia University before beginning his teaching at Gakushuin University. While researching in his specialized field of commercial law and corporate law, he has been active in comparative law studies as well, being a correspondent of UNIDROIT, and an associate member of the International Academy of Comparative Law (IACL). He has contributed to establishing contacts with Japanese law specialists outside of Japan on many occasions and is a program convenor in eastern Japan of the Australian Network for Japanese Law (ANJeL). Dr. Kozuka serves on the editorial board of the *Journal of Japanese Law* (*Zeitschrift für japanisches Recht*) published in Germany.

Arito Ono is senior economist at the Mizuho Research Institute. He also served as visiting lecturer at the Faculty of Economics at Saitama University (2008–2009), visiting professor at the Faculty of Commerce and Management at Hitotsubashi University (2009), senior economist at the Institute for Monetary and Economic Studies, Bank of Japan (2009–2011), and a member of working groups at the Financial System Council, Financial Services Agency (2011–2013). His main fields of research are banking and corporate finance, and he has published papers in the *Journal of Money, Credit, and Banking*, the *Journal of Banking & Finance*, and the *Journal of Financial Stability*. He received a B.A. in economics from the University of Tokyo and a Ph.D. in economics from Brown University.

Hirofumi Uchida is a professor of banking and finance at the Graduate School of Business Administration, Kobe University, Japan. He received his M.A. in economics in 1995 and his Ph.D. in economics in 1999, both from Osaka University. Prior to joining Kobe University in 2009, Professor Uchida was at the Kyoto Institute for Economic Research at Kyoto University and the Faculty of Economics at Wakayama University. He was also a visiting scholar at the Kelley School of Business, Indiana University, as a 2003 Fulbright Scholar. His research has been published in the *Journal of Financial Intermediation*, *Economica*, and the *Journal of Banking & Finance*, among others. He is also an associate editor of the *Journal of Money, Credit, and Banking*. His research interests focus on banking, financial institutions, and financial system architecture.

Iichiro Uesugi is an associate professor at the Institute of Economic Research of Hitotsubashi University and a faculty fellow at the Research Institute of the Economy, Trade and Industry. Before joining Hitotsubashi, he had worked for the Ministry of Economy, Trade and Industry of the Japanese government for 18 years. His main areas of research interest are banking, corporate finance, and firm dynamics. He has published papers in scholarly journals including the *Journal of Money, Credit, and Banking*, the *Journal of Banking & Finance*, the *Journal of Financial Stability*, and the *Journal of the Japanese and International Economies*. Professor Uesugi received a B.A. in economics from the University of Tokyo and a Ph.D. in economics from the University of California, San Diego.

Interfirm Relationships and Trade Credit in Japan: Evidence from Micro-Data

1 Data, Sample, and Methodology

In this paper, we describe the current status of interfirm relationships in Japan with a special emphasis on the trade credit between firms. To do so, we first need to clarify what kind of firms in Japan we report on. In this section, we describe the source of our data, and how we chose the sample firms that are used for the analysis in the subsequent sections. We also explain the methodology that we use when we report our findings in the sections below.

1.1 Data

1.1.1 Original Data and Initial Selection

Our original data are from the credit reports of Teikoku Databank Ltd. (hereafter called TDB). The TDB is one of the largest credit information providers in Japan. The main business of TDB is to regularly conduct credit research on firms, collect corporate information, and sell corporate and market data to customers. The TDB conducts its credit research on demand (i.e., in response to a request by a customer on a paid basis). It also conducts credit research on an unsolicited basis, which is the case for important, established, or large firms in Japan.

Because the coverage of TDB's research is so extensive, the original data include information on firms that are not comparable to ordinary firms in Japan. Thus, before proceeding to a full-scale analysis, we eliminate such firms. First, we eliminate firms that belong to not-for-profit industries, such as religious and educational bodies. Second, we also eliminate firms that belong to financial industries. Third, we do not cover firms whose corporate status is not ordinary. That is, we only retain joint stock companies (*kabusiki gaisha*), closely held (limited liability)

© The Author(s) 2015

H. Uchida et al., *Interfirm Relationships and Trade Credit in Japan*,
SpringerBriefs in Economics, DOI 10.1007/978-4-431-55187-4_1

companies (*yuugen gaisha*), sole proprietorships (*kojin gaisha*), medical associations (incorporated) (*iryou houjin*), cooperative partnerships (unincorporated) (*kyoudou/kyougyou kumiai*), limited and unlimited liability partnership companies (*goumei/gousi gaisha*), and limited liability partnerships (*yuugenn sekinin jigyo kumiai*).

1.1.2 Sample Period and Our "Cross-Sectional" Data

The original data include information from the TDB's credit reports from 2007 to 2010, which is basically the period that we refer to as "current." However, we do not use all of the data from this period, because during this period, quite a few sample firms appear multiple times in the data. Firms might have multiple data during the 2007–2010 period because TDB often receives multiple requests for credit research on the same firm to obtain up-to-date information. For those firms that TDB researched multiple times during the 2007–2010 period, the original data are pooled data, or are cross-sectional and time-series data.

However, because the time span is relatively short, and because the aim of this paper is to provide a snapshot of the whole picture of our sample firms, we construct a "cross-sectional" data set. That is, even if the original data include multiple records of a particular firm at different points of time during the 2007–2010 period, we use the latest record only and drop the others. This data set is "cross-sectional" because a firm appears only once in the 2007–2010 period.

1.1.3 Our Base Sample

Despite the selection processes above, we have an enormous number of firms in our sample. As we argue below, we have good reason to claim that our sample firms are representative of firms in Japan (see Sect. 2.2). However, the number of firms slightly changes depending on what information we focus on. This is because information from the credit research is sometimes incomplete, or missing. Thus, when we construct variables from the original credit research information, the number of observations changes from variable to variable due to "NA" or "unknown" observations for each variable.[1]

The information we can make use of most extensively is on the legal form of the firms (i.e., companies, closely held, etc.). We have such information for 386,826 firms in our sample. Also, we know the number of employees for 372,947 firms,

[1] In constructing variables, we tried to recover missing observations as much as possible by using information from other variables. For example, when a ratio that represents a composition of an item is unknown but the sum of the ratios of the other items is 100 %, the relevant ratio is set to zero.

and the credit score from the TDB (the evaluation of the firm by TDB on a 1–100 interval: see Sect. 2.1.6) for 367,224 firms. For the other variables, the number of observations is smaller than for these variables.

1.1.4 Financial Statement Data

The credit reports often accompany financial statement data as well, which TDB also obtains on demand or on an unsolicited basis. However, the number of observations for such data is significantly smaller than for credit reports. For example, we have information for the firms' dividend payment for only 143,720 firms, although still a large number. This is because firms, especially small- and medium-sized enterprises, do not record their business activities by creating financial statements. However, even when a firm does not have financial statements, we can recover some important figures, such as net current profit, from TDB's file on firm attributes. For example, the information on net current profit is available for 190,206 firms.[2]

1.2 Methodology

Using this data set, we report the current status of interfirm relationships in Japan. Our methodology is twofold. First, we report the descriptive statistics of each variable and thereby clarify the characteristics of the firms in Japan. In the tables below, we present the statistics as shown in Table 1. Some figures, such as fractions, are reported only in the text, but in that case we usually report the number of observations (i.e., N) that we used to calculate the figures. We additionally present frequency tables and figures where needed. All the monetary variables are in Japanese yen.

Table 1 Summary statistics to report

N	The number of observations
Mean	Arithmetical means
SD	Standard deviation
Min	Minimum
p1	1st percentile
p50	Median (50th percentile)
p99	99th percentile
Max	Maximum

2 Also, variables constructed from financial statement data sometimes take an extraordinary value. We have eliminated such data as outliers by dropping firms if variables' values fall into their largest and the smallest 0.1 % ranges.

Table 2 Base variables (variables to interact with other variables

Firm size	The number of employees
	Capital stock (capitalization)
	Operating revenue (=sales)
Firm performance	Net current profit
Creditworthiness	Credit score
	Capital asset ratio
	Interest-bearing debt operating revenue ratio

Second, to better grasp the characteristics of our sample firms, we also conduct a univariate analysis. That is, we split the sample firms into multiple categories based on the values of one or more variables, and calculate the descriptive statistics for each category. The variables used for this decomposition are hereafter called *base variables*. Table 2 contains the list of our base variables.

To represent the difference in firm characteristics depending on firm size, we use the number of employees, capital stock, and operating revenue (sales) to categorize variables. To examine whether firm characteristics differ depending on firm performance, we use net current profit as a base variable. We also use credit score (see Sect. 2.1.6), capital asset ratio, and interest-bearing debt operating revenue ratio to grasp the difference due to firm creditworthiness. We further expand this list of variables and use other variables, if doing so is necessary to deepen the analysis.

Because of the availability of the data, when we interact variables for a univariate analysis, the data points for the two variables might differ. Due to the "cross-sectional" nature of our data set from 2007 to 2010, there might be 4 years of a difference at the maximum when we pick up an arbitrary pair of two variables. To avoid comparing variables from points of time that are far apart, we limit our univariate analysis to the case when the interval of the data points is equal to, or smaller than, 36 months.

2 Firm Characteristics

2.1 Basic Characteristics of Our Sample Firms

2.1.1 Firm Size

Before reporting the current status of the interfirm relationships in Japan, we describe the characteristics of our sample firms by showing the descriptive statistics on their basic attributes. In this section, we report the descriptive statistics for the base variables (see Table 2) and other variables that enable us to characterize the image of our sample firms.

As a variable to comprehend firm size, we have information on the number of employees. As shown in Table 3, the mean number of employees for our sample firms is 49, while the median is 10. As this difference between mean and median implies, the distribution of firm size is skewed toward larger firms. However, the median indicates that more than half of the firms are small firms that hire less than ten employees. We also find that 6.03 % of the firms hire no employees. This finding means that these firms are run by their CEO only. We also find that more than 90 % of the firms (92.1 %) hire 100 or less employees (not reported in the table). This finding means that the majority of the firms are small- and medium-sized enterprises. However, the sample does contain 1,933 firms (0.52 %) that hire more than 1,000 employees. Large public companies are included in our sample.

To grasp the size distribution of our sample firms, we can also use information on the firms' capital stock (capitalization), as shown in Table 4. However, compared with Table 3, the number of observations is significantly reduced. This is because the information for capital stock is available from the firms' balance sheets, and there are many firms that do not have financial statements in our sample as is often the case for small- and medium-sized enterprises.

The average firm in our sample has 155 million yen (mean) or 15 million yen (median) of capital stock. For reference, in the original data we have observations with extreme numbers in their capital stock. If we do not drop the top and bottom 0.1 % of the firms in terms of their capitalization, then the mean figure almost doubles.

Yet another variable to indicate the size of our sample firms is operating revenue (=sales). Table 5 reports the descriptive statistics for the operating revenues of the sample firms. On average, sales of our sample firms are 3.5 billion yen, while the median is 0.5 billion. These figures are consistent with those in earlier tables that report that the majority of sample firms are small- and medium-sized enterprises.

Table 3 The number of employees (persons)

N	Mean	SD	Min	p1	p50	p99	Max
372,947	49.44663	426.1591	0	0	10	608	140,846

Table 4 Capital stock

N	Mean	SD	p50	Max
245,888	155,000,000	1,240,000,000	15,000,000	42,000,000,000

Table 5 Operating revenue

N	Mean	SD	p50	Max
183,321	3,510,000,000	18,600,000,000	515,000,000	588,000,000,000

Table 6 Net current profit

N	Mean	SD	Min	p50	Max
190,206	18,300,000	508,000,000	−12,400,000,000	1,865,000	12,300,000,000

Table 7 Dividend payment

N	Mean	SD	Min	p50	Max
143,720	17,700,000	172,000,000	0	0	5,650,000,000

2.1.2 Performance

As for firm performance, we have information on the firms' net current profit. As Table 6 shows, the sample firms, on average, earn 18.3 million yen (mean) or 1.87 million yen (median) of net current profit. The fact that the mean is much larger than the median indicates that there are a small number of firms that earn enormous profits compared with the other firms. Although this information is not reported in the table, we also find that 26.4 % of the firms earn negative net current profits. This finding might be surprising at first glance, but it is understandable when we take into account the fact that our sample firms are small- and medium-sized enterprises. Such firms often manipulate financial figures and report negative profits to avoid taxation.

Table 7 reports the summary statistics for the dividend payments of our sample firms. Dividend payments can only be made when the firm reports positive net current profits. And, even if a firm reports a positive net current profit, the dividend might not be made to retain the profits for internal reserves. As shown by the zero median, the majority of the sample firms do not pay a dividend. Specifically, we find that 79.7 % of the sample firms do not pay a dividend. However, the mean level of the dividend payments is 17.7 million yen, which means that there are some firms that pay a large amount of dividends.

2.1.3 Firm Attributes

Apart from the variables that are available from the firms' financial statements, one of the most important variables to characterize firms is their age. In our data set, we obtain the firm age from the date of the firms' establishment. The firm age is calculated as the number of years from the establishment to the sample period. As shown in Table 8, this information is available for a relatively large number of the firms (more than 370,000 firms). The average firm age is 26 (median) or 28 (mean) years. This average means that our sample firms are relatively old. However, this

Table 8 Firm age (years)

N	Mean	SD	Min	p1	p50	p99	Max
373,695	27.62588	17.66175	0	1	26	68	130

Table 9 Legal form of firms

	Freq.	Percent
Joint stock companies	298,386	77.14
Sole proprietorships	13,120	3.39
Limited and unlimited liability partnership companies	1,492	0.40
Closely held (limited liability) companies	68,178	17.62
Others	5,650	1.46
Total	386,826	100

old age does not mean that our sample has a bias. In Japan, firms are ordinarily old, partly reflecting the lack of active start-ups.

As explained above, the information on the legal form is available for most of the firms. Table 9 reports the distribution of our sample firms depending on their legal forms. In our sample, joint stock companies account for 77 %, and 17.6 % of the firms are closely held companies. Others include medical associations (incorporated), cooperative partnerships (unincorporated), and limited liability partnerships. The share of sole proprietorships is small in our sample. As mentioned below (Sect. 2.2), this share is even smaller than the whole firms (or population) in Japan.

2.1.4 Ownership Structure

The TDB's credit report contains information on the composition of firms' stockholders that reveals their ownership structure. Based on our calculation, we find that 64.3 % of the sample firms (N = 288,607) are owner-managed. The definition of owner-managed firms is that the majority of their capital stock is held by someone with the same surname as the representative (CEO).

We can also obtain images of the ownership with keiretsu ties. Although no direct information for a keiretsu relationship is available, we can specify whether firms accept equity investments from other companies that have effective decision-making power over the firms (e.g., subsidiaries, associate companies to which the equity methods are applicable, companies that belong to a group filing a consolidated tax return, etc.). According to our calculation, only 7.9 % (N = 27,183) of the total sample firms (N = 386,641) are keiretsu firms by this definition. We also find that among these keiretsu firms, 84 % of them have a dominant shareholder, which are probably their parent firms. The remaining keiretsu firms have no dominant shareholders, despite being considered to be affiliated with a keiretsu. However, the number of observations of these firms is small.

Finally, we can discern whether the sample firms are public or private. In our sample, only 0.9 % of the firms (3,394 out of 386,826) are listed firms. This percentage means that private companies are the majority.

2.1.5 Region and Industry

To show the geographical distribution of our sample firms, Table 10 decomposes the firms depending on their location. Specifically, we group the firms by the prefecture that they are located in. There are 47 prefectures in Japan, and 21.8 % of the sample firms are located in the Tokyo prefecture, the capital of Japan. The second largest prefecture in terms of the number of our sample firms is the Osaka prefecture, which is the economic center of the west business areas in Japan. Osaka contains 9.9 % of our sample firms. The Aichi prefecture (its capital is Nagoya city), the third largest metropolitan area in Japan, is next with 5.7 % of the sample firms. As for the other prefectures, 5.0 % are in the Kanagawa prefecture, which is

Table 10 Region (prefecture)

Prefecture	Freq.	Percentage	Prefecture	Freq.	Percentage
Hokkaido	16,823	4.35	Shiga	2,854	0.74
Aomori	3,450	0.89	Kyoto	7,506	1.94
Iwate	3,320	0.86	Osaka	38,252	9.89
Miyagi	5,880	1.52	Hyogo	13,420	3.47
Akita	2,753	0.71	Nara	2,731	0.71
Yamagata	3,028	0.78	Wakayama	2,328	0.60
Fukushima	5,071	1.31	Tottori	1,312	0.34
Ibaraki	6,947	1.80	Shimane	1,658	0.43
Tochigi	4,640	1.20	Okayama	5,512	1.42
Gumma	5,643	1.46	Hiroshima	8,124	2.10
Saitama	14,581	3.77	Yamaguchi	3,545	0.92
Chiba	10,768	2.78	Tokushima	2,035	0.53
Tokyo	84,179	21.76	Kagawa	3,381	0.87
Kanagawa	19,206	4.97	Ehime	3,536	0.91
Niigata	6,350	1.64	Kochi	1,970	0.51
Toyama	3,317	0.86	Fukuoka	13,923	3.60
Ishikawa	3,556	0.92	Saga	2,012	0.52
Fukui	2,799	0.72	Nagasaki	3,041	0.79
Yamanashi	2,784	0.72	Kumamoto	3,963	1.02
Nagano	6,846	1.77	Oita	2,821	0.73
Gifu	5,307	1.37	Miyazaki	2,929	0.76
Shizuoka	10,149	2.62	Kagoshima	3,448	0.89
Aichi	21,880	5.66	Okinawa	2,953	0.76
Mie	4,295	1.11			
			Total	386,826	100.00

Table 11 Industry

Industry	Freq.	Percentage
Agriculture	1,629	0.42
Forestry and hunting	157	0.04
Fishery	476	0.12
Mining	572	0.15
Construction	69,458	18.08
Manufacturing	73,482	19.13
Wholesale	89,367	23.27
Retail and restaurant	47,227	12.30
Finance and insurance	258	0.07
Real estate	14,151	3.68
Transportation and telecommunication	19,529	5.08
Electricity, gas, water, and heat supply	188	0.05
Services	67,590	17.60
Public services (not classified as others)	1	0.00
Unclassifiables	4	0.00
Total	384,089	100.00

next to Tokyo and its capital is Yokohama city, and 4.4 % are in the Hokkaido prefecture, which is the northern most and has the largest area in Japan (its capital is Sapporo city). For all of the other prefectures, the percentage is smaller than 4 %.

Table 11 shows the number of firms when we decompose them by industry (N = 384,089). The top five industries in our sample are: Wholesale (23.3 %), Manufacturing (19.1 %), Construction (18.1 %), Services (17.6 %), and Retail and restaurants (12.3 %). As explained earlier, we eliminate financial firms, but as shown in this table, some of them get through the sample selection process. Examples of these firms are credit card companies and agents for insurance.

2.1.6 Credit Risk

The TDB evaluates the firms in their database, which is summarized as a *score* (*hyoten* in Japanese). This score takes an integer value on a 1–100 scale. It evaluates the soundness of the firm's management, the firm's repayment ability, and whether others can safely trade with the firm, from a third-party viewpoint. The score is calculated based on a quantitative evaluation of the financial figures, past performances, the operating history of the firms, and the qualitative evaluation of the firms by researchers (including the evaluation of their managers (CEOs)). This

Table 12 Credit score

N	Mean	SD	Min	p1	p50	p99	Max
367,224	47.52415	7.538036	1	30	48	66	88

score is unsolicited, that is, the relevant firms do not pay to be rated. The TDB's score is one of their key products, and the firms in Japan often purchase information on the scores of potential trade partners when they consider doing business with them. The TDB notes that the average score fluctuates, depending on business conditions, in a procyclical manner.

As Table 12 shows, the average score is around 50 (47.5 (in mean) and 48 (in median)). Although the score is procyclical, we can consider that a firm with a score of 50 is an average firm.

2.1.7 Financial Ratios

Finally, we show in Table 13 the summary statistics for different financial ratios that are calculated based on the financial statements. As mentioned earlier, the number of observations is significantly smaller than those in previous tables because the financial statement information is not available for all of the sample firms.

From Table 13, we can confirm the following facts:

1. The mean capital asset ratio (capital stock/total asset) is 21.1 %, and its median is 21.7 %. Not reported, we also find that 13.6 % of the firms have excess debt (capital asset ratio less than zero). This finding is in contradiction with the 26.4 % of our sample firms having negative net current profits (Sect. 2.1.2), which is larger than 13.6 %. The (seeming) inconsistency stems from the difference in the number of sample firms, or in the data availability.
2. Loans (Borrowing) from financial institutions accounts for 49.8 % (mean), or 38.3 % (median), of the firms' balance sheets. We also find that there are some firms with no borrowing (7.3 % of the sample), and other firms with excessive borrowing (those with the ratio greater than 1: 2.69 % of the sample). To further examine the difference in the borrowing rates by region, we interact this ratio with regional dummies. We find that Okinawa (33.6 %), Nara (35.2 %), Kagawa (36.1 %), Wakayama (36.3 %), and Nagasaki (37.2 %) are the bottom five prefectures with a low average borrowing rate, while Gifu (85.3 %), Gunma (82.6 %), Tochigi (76.7 %), Saga (74.2 %), and Kumamoto (67.4 %) are the top five prefectures (N = 150,883).
3. The mean operating profit operating revenue ratio (=operating profit/sales) is zero. Its median, 1.1 %, is also small. These figures appear smaller than expected, but they could be due to the fact that our sample period covers the economic slump after the global financial crisis. However, the small figures could also be the result of the firms' efforts to reduce taxes through accounting manipulation, because the firms are taxed only when they are in surplus.

Table 13 Financial ratios

	N	Mean	SD	Min	p1	p50	p99	Max
1. Capital/total asset	247,337	0.211	0.506	−9.333	−1.608	0.217	0.927	0.990
2. Loans from financial institutions/total asset	150,931	0.498	3.973	0.000	0.000	0.383	1.399	280.597
3. Operating profit/operating revenue	182,866	0.000	0.178	−6.168	−0.414	0.011	0.232	0.542
4. Interest bearing debt/(operating revenue/12)	165,196	5.738	13.360	0.000	0.000	3.054	52.010	374.022
5. Interest payments/total debt	157,041	0.034	0.077	0.000	0.000	0.025	0.221	2.616

4. As for the interest bearing debt to operating revenue ratio, its mean is 5.74 and the median is 3.05. These numbers imply that, by using its own income, an average firm can repay their debt in 5.7 or 3 months (in the absence of operating costs).
5. The final financial ratio, the interest payment to total debt ratio, is a proxy for an average annual interest rate. Note that this ratio includes interest rates for securities (debt obligations) other than bank loans, so it does not necessarily equal the interest rate paid for bank debt. Its mean is 3.4 % and its median is 2.5 %. We also find that this ratio is zero, meaning no interest payments, for 1.4 % of the firms. There are a few reasons for this zero interest rate. For example, the debt might be from the owner-manager or family members. Also, some firms might be unable to repay debt. Further, even if the repayment was made, it might be made in a different year.

When examining interest rates in Japan, the Interest Rate Restrictions Law (IRRL) has an important effect. The IRRL places caps on the rate of interest to be accrued on a loan at 20 % per annum if the principal is less than 100,000 yen, 18 % if the principal is 100,000 yen or more but less than 1 million yen, and 15 % if the principal is 1 million yen or more. Any agreement on the interest in excess of these caps is null and void.

As shown in Table 13, the maximum of the interest payments to total debt ratio is 261.6 %, which is greater than the 20 % cap. However, this ratio does not imply that the law is ineffective. The ratio is calculated based on financial statement numbers, that is, it is calculated using interest payments in income statements that are flow variables, and the total debt in balance sheets that is a stock variable. The ratio might thus be a poor proxy for the actual interest rate due to the mismatch between the numerator and the denominator.

2.2 Comparison with Other Surveys

To understand how representative our sample firms are, we compare the summary statistics from the TDB database with those of several government corporate surveys. These surveys include the Census of Establishments and Firms (hereafter called the Census), which is the census survey of all the firms (incorporations and proprietorships) operating in Japan; and the annual Basic Survey of Small and Medium Enterprises (hereafter called the Basic SME Survey), which describes SME characteristics in Japan.

In terms of the number of firms, the 2006 Census reports that the number of corporations in Japan is 1,493,258. The maximum number of corporations in our TDB database is 373,706 (excluding the number of proprietorships from the entire sample). The coverage of the TDB database is indeed limited, but it covers a sizable portion of the total population. Especially, while the Census includes a large number of sole proprietorships in their sample, they account for only 3.39 % of our sample firms (see Table 9). Also note that our sample firms are those that survived our sample selection criteria (see Sect. 1.1).

Turning to industry composition, the industry with the largest share in the Census is Construction (18.5 %), which is followed by Retail (17.6 %), Manufacturing (17.1 %), Services (14.0 %), and Wholesale (11.6 %). In our data set Wholesale dominates the others at 23.3 %, which is followed by Manufacturing (19.1 %), Construction (18.1 %), Services (17.6 %), and Retail and restaurant (12.3 %) (see Table 11). By comparison, wholesale and manufacturing industries have a relatively larger share in the TDB database than they do in the Census.

Regarding the firm size (employee size), the median firm in the 2006 Census employs four or less employees. As we have already shown above (Table 3), the median number of employees is ten in the TDB database. The TDB database has a sufficiently large number of small firms for analysis, but its size distribution is somewhat skewed toward the right when compared with the population of the Census.

Finally, regarding the average (mean) capital ratio, the ratio in the 2009 Basic SME Survey (27.7 %) is higher than that in our database (21.1 %: Table 13). This difference suggests that the firms in the TDB data base are more dependent on liabilities (including bank loans) than those in the Basic SME Survey.

2.3 *Univariate Analysis of the Borrowing Ratio and the Interest Rate*

To further characterize our sample firms, we conduct some univariate analysis on two of the financial variables reported in Table 13: the borrowing ratio and the interest rate. First, we break down the borrowing ratio (loans from financial

Table 14 Borrowing ratio by the number of banks

# of banks	N	Mean	SD	Min	p50	Max
1	12,197	0.380439	3.322464	0	0.194805	227.2727
2	28,508	0.458659	4.285322	0	0.286530	270.4342
3	34,401	0.472492	3.689403	0	0.349275	264.1829
4	27,983	0.532851	4.739675	0	0.397562	280.5974
5	18,772	0.551503	4.093062	0	0.433202	242.8941
6	11,478	0.518996	2.827121	0	0.466544	225.9816
7	7,006	0.555256	3.868429	0	0.485639	260.2589
8	4,116	0.551445	2.910753	0	0.500524	183.5441
9	2,417	0.617612	5.596556	0	0.512654	275.3903
10	1,464	0.562806	1.757387	0	0.524867	67.1597
11 or more	2,511	0.556256	0.545585	0	0.541727	18.0219
Total	150,853	0.497596	3.973888	0	0.382732	280.5974

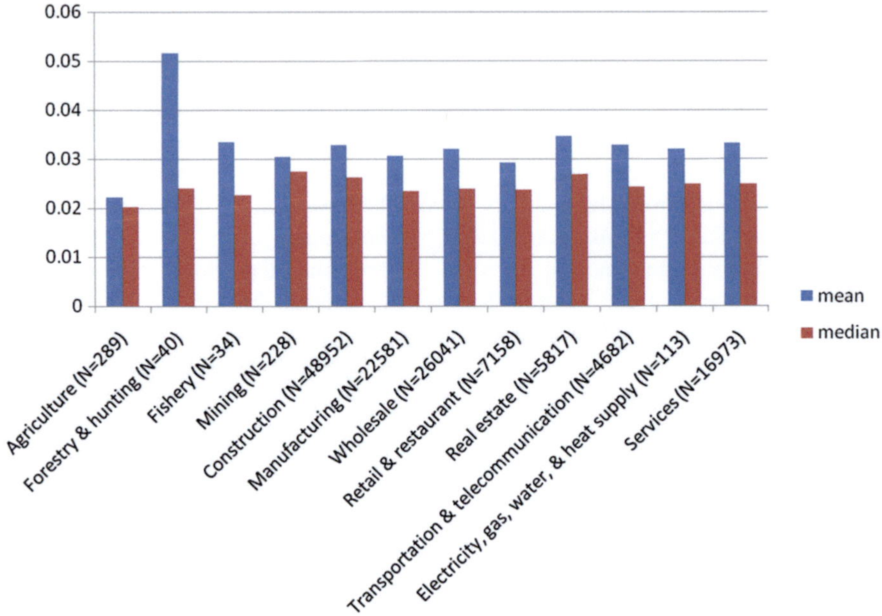

Fig. 1 Interest rate by industry

institutions over total asset) by the number of banks. Table 14 shows that the median ratio (p50) is smoothly increasing, which might reflect the firms' and/or the banks' risk diversification, or a greater ability of more creditworthy firms to borrow from more banks. The positive association between the two variables is also present, but less clearly, in the case of the mean.

Second, we compare the interest rate (interest payment/(long-term + short-term borrowing)) by industry (N = 132,908). The results (Fig. 1) show that the mean rate is between 2.9 and 3.5 % for most industries. When compared with the other industries, Forestry and hunting (5.17 %) and Agriculture (2.22 %) exhibit somewhat extraordinary values, but we should take into account the fact that the number of observations for these industries is small. The median rate exhibits no industry variation. The rates range within a small interval from 2.02 (Agriculture) to 2.74 % (Mining).

Third, we break down the interest rate by firm size (the number of employees). As shown in Table 15, we find that the mean interest rate only slightly increases with firm size. However, when we focus on the median, it shows an inverted-U shape. As for the slight increase, it might be due to more borrowing from CEOs or relatives (which is presumably interest-free) for smaller firms. Similar relationships exist when we break down the interest rate by credit score, capital stock, and operating revenue, and to a lesser extent when broken down by the capital asset ratio and the net current profit, although these results are not reported in the table.

These findings seem to indicate that larger, more creditworthy, and better-performing firms pay higher interest rates on average (in means). However, the standard deviation is also greater for larger, more creditworthy, and better-performing

Table 15 Interest rate by the number of employees

x = # of employees	N	Mean (%)	SD (%)	Min (%)	p50 (%)	Max (%)
x = 0	3,317	3.050	5.440	−0.820	2.350	142.6
0 < x ≤ 3	14,506	2.960	5.760	0.000	2.370	217.1
3 < x ≤ 6	17,479	3.060	5.050	0.000	2.530	212.8
6 < x ≤ 10	18,067	3.220	5.780	0.000	2.600	196.0
10 < x ≤ 20	25,948	3.310	6.390	−1.550	2.610	253.4
20 < x ≤ 50	26,704	3.320	6.800	0.000	2.530	261.6
50 < x ≤ 100	12,106	3.240	7.010	−0.230	2.370	253.0
100 < x ≤ 300	9,547	3.260	7.670	0.000	2.280	247.8
300 < x ≤ 1,000	3,480	3.640	10.540	0.000	2.120	258.3
1,000 < x	1,157	3.850	13.500	0.000	1.830	236.2
Total	132,311	3.220	6.550	−1.550	2.480	261.6

firms. Taken together, our findings mean that a small number of very large, creditworthy, and better-performing firms are paying very high interest rates. In terms of the median interest rates, it is the intermediate firms that pay higher interest rates.

Fourth, we break down the interest rate by prefecture (N = 133,127). The results (Fig. 2) show some cross-region dispersion in the interest rates. From the left to the right, Fig. 2 shows the mean and the median interest rate from north to south

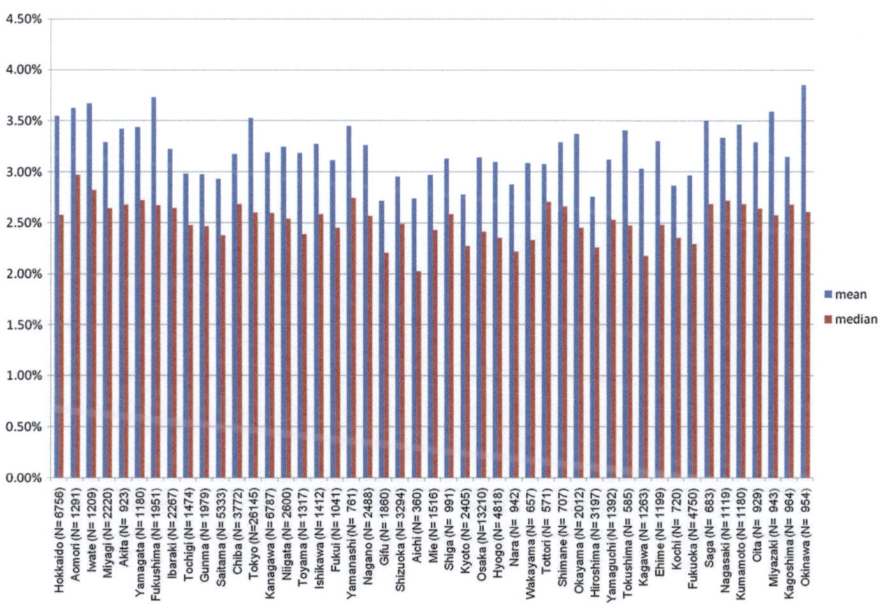

Fig. 2 Interest rate by prefecture

prefectures. The top five prefectures that have the highest interest rates are Okinawa (3.86 %), Fukushima (3.73 %), Iwate (3.67 %), Aomori (3.63 %), and Miyazaki (3.59 %) in the mean. In terms of the median, the top five are Aomori (2.97 %), Iwate (2.82 %), Yamanashi (2.74 %), Yamagata (2.72 %), and Nagasaki (2.72 %). The bottom five prefectures that have the lowest interest rates are Gifu (2.72 %), Aichi (2.74 %), Hiroshima (2.76 %), Kochi (2.86 %), and Nara (2.88 %) in the mean; and Aichi (2.02 %), Kagawa (2.18 %), Gifu (2.21 %), Nara (2.22 %), and Hiroshima (2.26 %) in the median.

Kyoto and Aichi prefectures are anecdotally considered as low interest rate prefectures due to harsh bank competition, while prefectures in the Tohoku area (including Aomori, Iwate, and Yamagata) are considered as high interest rate ones. In our sample, the "Aichi rate" and the "Tohoku rate" are indeed observed, but the "Kyoto rate" is not. An investigation into the reasons for such regional differences might be interesting; for example, bank competition, business condition, industry distribution, etc. However, by its definition, the interest rate is not necessarily equal to the interest rate for bank borrowing.

Finally, we break down the interest rate by the number of banks that the firms transact with (N = 132,727). The results (not shown in a table) indicate that the mean rate does not differ depending on the number of banks: the rate takes a value between 3.05 and 3.38 %. In terms of the median, the rate monotonically increases from 2.26 % (for firms that transact with a single bank) to 2.84 % (for firms that transact with 11 or more banks). To the extent that this increase is significant (statistically and/or economically), it is puzzling because bank competition should reduce interest rates. It might be the case that financially constrained firms try to borrow from more banks. Alternatively, it might be that the number of banks simply represents firm size; large firms borrow for longer maturity, and long maturity loans are expensive. The other possible reason is that firms borrowing from more banks are more risky. This final interpretation is consistent with our finding earlier that the firms that transact with more banks have a higher borrowing ratio (Table 14).

3 Interfirm Trade and Trade Credit

3.1 Trade Counterparts

In this section, we report the current status of interfirm trade in Japan, with a special emphasis on trade credit. Because our data set is huge and unique, our findings should capture the real state of interfirm transactions in Japan.

We begin our analysis on the number of trade counterparts for firms in Japan. Table 16 shows the descriptive statistics for the number of suppliers from which a firm purchases, and the number of customers that a firm sells to. Not only firms but also individuals are included in these figures, although the TDB explains that the unspecified (i.e., too large a) number of (retail) customers is not included in the

Table 16 The number of suppliers and customers

	N	Mean	SD	Min	p1	p50	p99	Max
# of suppliers	324,734	47.243	247.761	0	1	20	400	70,000
# of customers	241,335	278.465	1,814.865	0	1	40	3,500	90,504

Table 17 Degree of dependence (%) on main suppliers

	N	Mean	SD	Min	p1	p50	p99	Max
Main suppliers total	57,315	61.292	27.672	0.022	6.534	60.544	100	100
Top supplier only	58,185	49.192	29.302	0.006	5	45	100	100

number of customers. As the table shows, an average sample firm purchases from 47 (in mean) or 20 (in median) suppliers, and sells to 278.5 (in mean) or 40 (in median) customers. The number of customers is larger than that of suppliers. If we interact the numbers of suppliers and customers (N = 224,304), the latter gradually increases with the former, and increases at an increasing rate.

The TDB identifies firms' *main* suppliers and the *top* supplier, although the definition of the "main" or "top" is based on their subjective evaluation and is thus unclear. We also have information about the average monthly purchases from the main suppliers. We can therefore calculate the degree of dependence on the main suppliers as the ratio of total purchases from main suppliers and the total monthly purchases (which is recorded as the cost of goods sold). Table 17 shows the descriptive statistics for this degree of dependence on the main suppliers. We find that on average 60 % of the purchases are from main suppliers (no significant difference is found between the mean and the median). Table 17 also shows the degree of dependence on the top supplier. Compared with that on the main suppliers, the degree on the top supplier is smaller at 45 (in the median) or 50 % (in the mean).

We similarly calculate the degree of dependence on the main customers or on the top customer based on sales information. The descriptive statistics are shown in Table 18. We find that about 70–80 % of the sales are to main customers. Also, the sales to the top customer account for about 60 % of the total sales.

Table 18 Degree of dependence (%) on main customers

	N	Mean	SD	Min	p1	p50	p99	Max
Main total	92,539	69.514	29.362	0.004	7	80	100	100
Top only	92,981	58.099	32.102	0.003	5	60	100	100

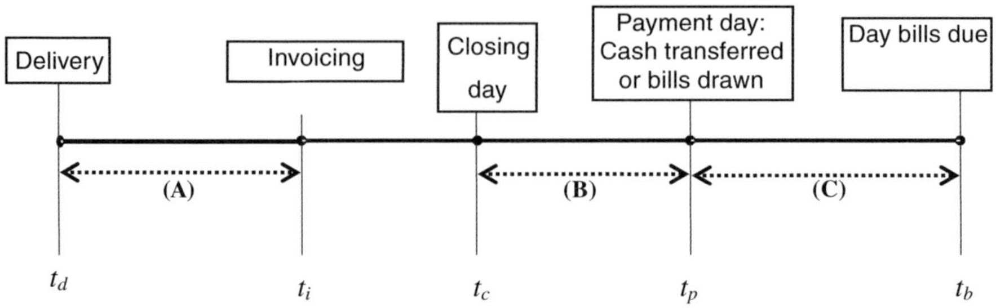

Fig. 3 Trade credit practice in Japan

3.2 Trade Credit Practice in Japan

The practice of trade credit in Japan is somewhat similar to that in other countries, but it also is unique.[3] Figure 3 illustrates how corporate payments typically proceed in Japan from a buyer's viewpoint. Suppose that a transaction deal is done, and that the product is delivered (or service is provided) to the buyer at $t = t_d$. It then takes some time (period (A)) for the seller to complete the necessary paperwork, before issuing an invoice and presenting it to the buyer ($t = t_i$). Because the payment for the product (or the service) has not yet been made, the buyer (seller) records accounts payable (receivable) on its book, which is usually made either on t_d or on t_i. *Accounts receivable* (*payable*) [*kaikake-kin* (*urikake-kin*) in Japanese] are an open account credit (debt). An open account credit is the most common form of trade credit in many countries. The evidence of a buyer's indebtedness is the seller's entry of the transaction in the sales ledger for that customer (Emery and Ariga 1996).

Payment is not made at the time when the firm receives an invoice. It is conventional for firms in Japan to have their own *closing day* (*shime-bi* in Japanese) ($t = t_c$) in each month (e.g., the end of month). Until the closing day, the firms accumulate their debts and credits that have emerged during the month and settle the balance vis-à-vis each seller on the closing day. A closing day helps firms to reduce transaction costs from processing multiple payments.

The two most commonly used methods of payment in Japan are a bank transfer and a promissory bill.[4] And depending on what method of payment the buyer uses, the day a seller receives cash (i.e., the payment is settled) differs. Irrespective of which method is used, a day that is typically called the *payment day* (*shiharai-bi* in Japanese) ($t = t_p$) comes a certain number of days after the closing day (e.g., 30 days). If a buyer makes a payment by *bank transfer* (*ginko furikomi* in Japanese),

---

[3] The explanation that follows borrows much from Uchida et al. (2010).

[4] Interviews with practitioners suggest that the use of checks as a method of payment on the payment day is very rare. As checks are immediately refundable, they are used as an alternative to immediate cash payment (i.e., not for credit payment).

the buyer electronically transfers cash from his/her own demand deposit account to the seller's account on or before this payment day. Once the transfer is made, the seller can withdraw the cash at any time.

However, firms in Japan also use another method of payment, *promissory bills* (promissory notes, or *yakusoku tegata* in Japanese).[5] In the case of promissory bills, the payment day is not a day when the seller does (or can) receive cash. Rather, it is the day when the seller receives (and the buyer "pays" by) a *paper-based promissory bill* that the buyer issues. The bill is refundable only at or after its due day (*kessai-bi*) ($t = t_b$), which usually comes a few months after the payment day (period (C)). At or after the due day, the seller deposits the bill at a bank; the bank takes the bill to a regional clearinghouse; and the bill, together with other bills collected on that day, is settled and cleared through the bank settlement system.[6] In principle, it is only after this process that the seller can receive cash. This process means that although t_p is called a "payment" day, the actual payment is not made on t_p when a promissory bill is used. Due to this time difference, the maturity of promissory bills is typically longer than that of a bank transfer by a few months.[7]

Similar to the case of a bank transfer, until the payment day, payments through promissory bills are recorded on the buyer's (seller's) book as accounts payable (receivable). However, once a bill is issued, the accounts payable (receivable) are turned into *bills payable* (*receivable*) [*shiharai-tegata* (*uketori-tegata*) in Japanese] on the books, and the bill serves as evidence of a buyer's indebtedness.

When promissory bills are used, the seller can also liquidate them by having a bank discount them, or use the bills as collateral for a loan (as long as the bank agrees to do so), instead of waiting to cash them on the due day. Bill discounting (*tegata waribiki* in Japanese) by banks is one of the main banking services through which banks in Japan earn commissions.[8] Also, a seller can endorse promissory bills and use them as his/her own method of payment to its sellers (as long as the sellers accept). The relatively extensive use of promissory bills in Japan might be linked to the institutional framework that facilitates the liquidation of them in these manners.

However, when discounting or endorsing promissory bills, the bank or the endorsee has recourse against the seller when the original buyer defaults. This means that even after the liquidation, the seller still assumes all the credit risk of the original buyers. Also, the methods of discounting promissory bills do not change the duration of the original credit extended to the buyers. So, regardless of whether

---

[5] Whether to use a bank transfer or a promissory bill is determined when the original deal is done ($t = t_d$).

[6] Regional clearing houses are run by banks in the relevant regions and are open every business day.

[7] Promissory bills and checks share similar characteristics. Both are paper-based and are cashed at a bank. One important difference is that checks can be cashed on demand, but promissory bills cannot be cashed until their due day.

[8] See Matsumura and Ryser (1995) and Miwa and Ramseyer (2008) for details on these methods of bills discounting.

a bill is liquidated or not, the seller assumes all the credit risk of the original buyer until the due date of the bill.

A unique feature of promissory bills is that there is a strong enforcement mechanism for payment. When a buyer (borrower) defaults on a promissory bill, the buyer's bank creates a *dishonor report* (*fuwatari joho* in Japanese) that is circulated to all of the member banks of the clearinghouse. Another default during a six-month period triggers a suspension of banking transactions by the member banks for 2 years. Such a firm cannot survive, because most of the banks participate in every clearinghouse (either directly or indirectly through agent banks). This serves as a strong enforcement mechanism for payment using promissory bills.[9]

The use of promissory bills as a method of payment is not unique to Japan. For example, they are also used in a few other Asian countries such as Korea and Taiwan.[10] Moreover, a similar method of payment, *bills of exchange*, was used in the United Kingdom until the nineteenth century (Bates and Hally 1982, p. 168). In the past, firms in the United States also have used bills as a last resort to obtain credit when encountering serious financial difficulties (Steffen 1964, p. 724). Nowadays, these methods are not extensively used for domestic transactions in either country.[11] However, bills of exchange are still frequently used for international transactions.

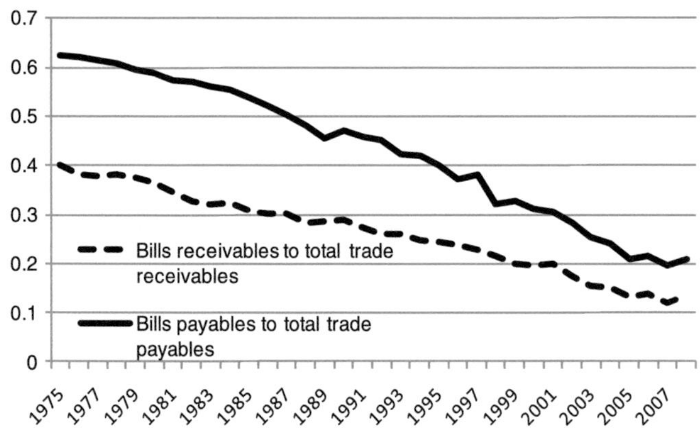

Fig. 4 The ratio of promissory bills in total trade credit

[9] Checks written on checking-account deposits are also subject to the same penalty, but as checks can be cashed anytime after their issuance, they are used as a cash-equivalent.

[10] In Korea, about 30–35 % (35–40 %) of trade credit during the period of 1990–1995 consisted of bills receivable (payable) (Bank of Korea, *Financial Statement Analysis*, various years). Since 1996, the breakdown of trade credit is no longer reported.

[11] The present domestic U.S. payment system is distinctive from those in other OECD countries with its greater reliance on paper checks (James and Weiman 2010).

That being said, the use of promissory bills in Japan has been declining steadily over the past few decades. Figure 4 (adopted from Uchida et al. 2010) shows the ratio of the outstanding amount of bills issued to the total amount of trade credit.[12] We find that bills receivable and bills payable are both steadily declining. To investigate the cause of this decline, despite the strong enforcement mechanism for repayment attached to promissory bills, might be an interesting research topic.[13]

3.3 Method of Payment (for Firms as Payers)

3.3.1 Composition

The TDB data provide us with information about the payment methods that the sample firms usually use when they make a payment to their suppliers. We know information on five such methods: (1) cash (including bank transfer, wire transfer, and checks), (2) promissory bills, (3) endorsement of promissory bills (that the firm received as a method of payment from other firms), (4) setting-off (canceling out with trade receivables), and/or (5) prepayment. However, category (1) does not specify when the cash is paid. Thus, it includes payment by cash and by checks at the time of the delivery and does not necessarily represent payment on account. However, below we find that almost all firms make this payment on account, so category (1) does represent credit payment. Category (2) (promissory bills) is the other method of credit payment in Japan. In the case of (5) prepayment, it is the seller that owes debt to the buyer.

From the TDB data, we know whether firms use each of these methods of payment. If we calculate the fractions of firms that use these five methods of payment for their payment (for any non-zero amount, multiple answers are allowed), they are respectively (1) 99.81 % (out of N = 367,604), (2) 33.63 % (N = 367,489), (3) 10.13 % (N = 367,423), (4) 2.38 % (N = 367,393), and (5) 0.21 % (N = 367,378). Almost all of our sample firms use cash, so the most dominant method of payment is cash. We also find that 59.74 % of the firms use cash only when they make payments. However, the other firms use cash together with the other methods of payment. Also, 681 firms (0.19 %) never use cash.

Next, Table 19 shows the descriptive statistics for the fraction of payment made through each of the methods of payment. Note that these fractions are different from the fractions of firms that use (non-zero amount of) each payment method, which we have reported in the previous paragraph. Rather than such fractions of users, this table reports the share of each method in the total amount of payment made. From this table, we again find (in a different form) that cash is a dominant method of

[12] The source of the data is the Financial Statements Statistics of Corporations by Industry from the Ministry of Finance: all industries and all sizes.

[13] Anecdote indicates that high transactional costs including stamp taxes contributed the decline.

Table 19 Fractions of methods used to make payments

Method	N	Mean	SD	Min	p1	p50	p99	Max
(1) Cash	367,604	81.890	27.597	0	10	100	100	100
(2) Promissory bills	367,489	14.357	24.993	0	0	0	90	100
(3) Endorsement	367,423	2.956	11.209	0	0	0	60	100
(4) Setting-off	367,393	0.689	5.733	0	0	0	25	100
(5) Prepayment	367,378	0.099	2.624	0	0	0	0	100

payment, i.e., in terms of the fraction of its usage in the total payment. As shown in this table, cash is used by firms for 81.9 % (in mean) or 100 % (in median) of the payments.

In contrast, Table 19 shows that Promissory bills account for 14 % of the payment. If we exclude those firms that never use any bills, and categorize the remaining firms (N = 123,604) (for each 5 % interval), promissory bills account for 6–10 % of the payments for 10 % of these firms, 16–20 % for 10 % of them, 26–30 % for 11 % of them, 46–50 % for 12 % of them, and 66–70 % for 10 % of them. The percentages for all the other categories are less than 10 %. Thus, promissory bills are rarely used as the sole method of payment, but they are not a minor method because they are used together with the other methods of payment (mostly cash).

As for the other three methods of payment, Table 19 shows that they are rarely used. The fraction of each is less than 3 %. From an additional analysis, we find that the endorsement of the other firms' promissory bills and setting-off are secondary methods of payment. The fraction of each of these two methods is less than 20 % for more than half of the firms that use them (N = 37,209 for endorsement and N = 8,749 for setting-off). In contrast, prepayment might be used as a dominant payment method when it is used. Out of 786 firms that use a non-zero fraction of prepayment, 11.96 % of them (N = 94) use prepayment only. However, another 53.31 % (N = 419) use prepayment only less than 40 %.

3.3.2 Univariate Analysis (1): Cash

We next check whether the use of a different method of payment differs depending on different firm characteristics. When broken down by industry (N = 367,100), the median cash ratio is 100 % for most industries (see Fig. 5). The exceptions are Mining (70 %), Construction (95 %), Manufacturing (70 %), and Wholesale (95 %). The mean ratios exhibit a similar pattern with Mining, Manufacturing, Wholesale, and Construction being the top four industries that do not use cash. In contrast, Real-estate firms depend greatly on cash.

When interacted with firm size (the number of employees), the cash ratio exhibits a U-shape (N = 362,729) (see Fig. 6). That is, large as well as small firms use more

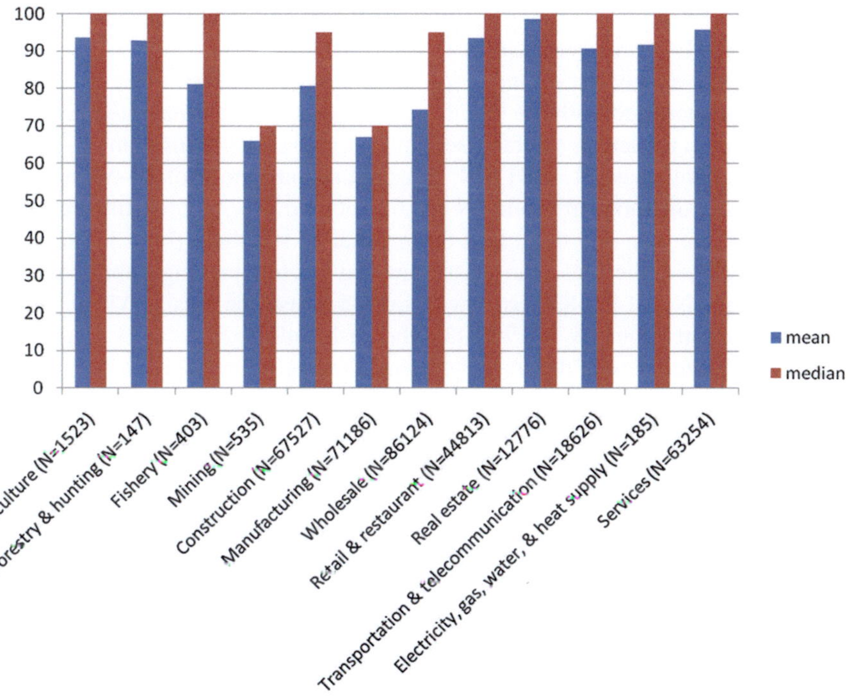

Fig. 5 Cash ratio (%) by industry

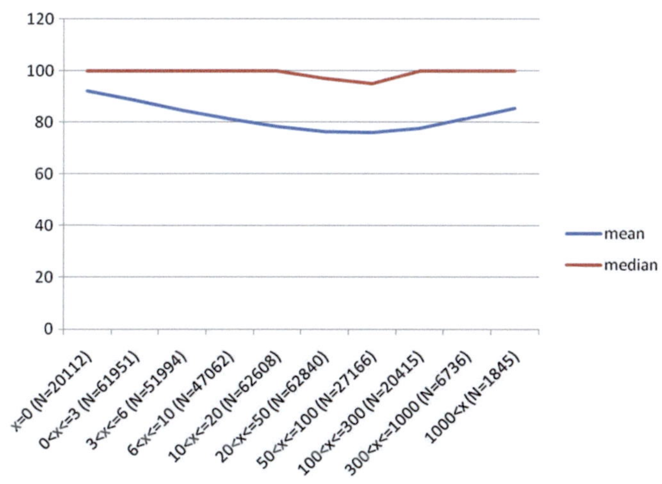

Fig. 6 Cash ratio (%) by firm size (x = the number of employees)

cash, but intermediate firms use less (e.g., mean = 76.2 % and median = 95 % for firms with 50–100 employees).

A similar U-shaped mean and a V-shaped median are also observed when the cash ratio is interacted with the credit score (N = 362,168: firms rated between 60 and 65 use cash the least), capital asset ratio (N = 233,319: firms with 20–30 % use the least), capital stock (N = 231,824: firms with capital stock of 20–50 million yen use the least), operating revenue (N = 162,166: firms with operating revenue of 300–500 million yen use the least), the number of suppliers (N = 321,638: firms with 100–300 suppliers use the least), and the interest bearing debt to operating revenue ratio (N = 141,683: firms with ratio 5–8 use the least). When interacted with net current profit (N = 170,143), the cash ratio exhibits a W-shape and is higher for categories with the smallest losses, the largest losses, or the largest gains.

3.3.3 Univariate Analysis (2): Promissory Bills

Turning to promissory bills, Fig. 7 show the differences in their usage by industry (N = 366,985). We find that promissory bills are extensively used in Mining (20 %) and Manufacturing (10 %). In means, in addition to these industries (28.6 % for Mining and 25.5 % for Manufacturing), Wholesale (19.8 %), Fishery (17.0 %), and Construction (15.8 %) use relatively more promissory bills. However, small observations for Mining and Fishery should also be taken into account.

Because more than half of our sample firms use cash only, it is interesting to examine the usage of promissory bills by the other (non cash-only) firms. As shown in Fig. 8, if we exclude firms that make payment by cash only, the means and

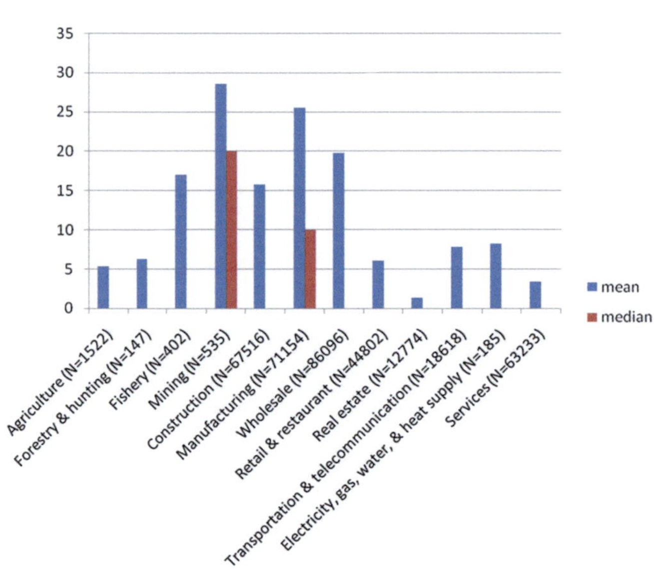

Fig. 7 Bill ratio (%) by industry

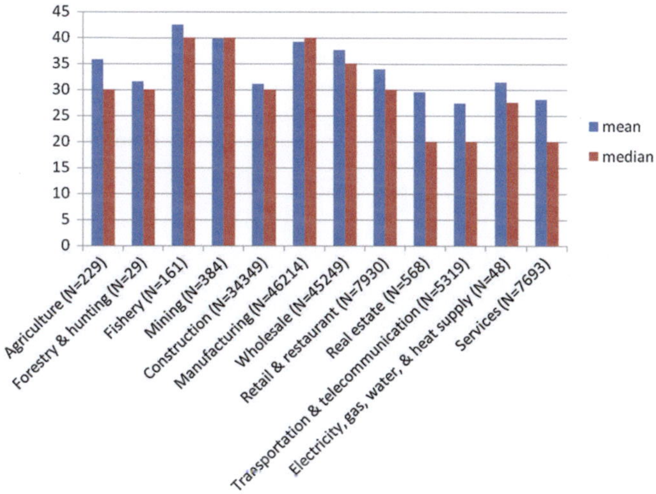

Fig. 8 Bill ratio (%) by industry (excluding cash only firms)

medians naturally increase (N = 148,173). Among those firms that use promissory bills, the bills are used for a non-negligible fraction of their payments. Real estate (N = 568), Transportation & telecommunication (N = 5,319), and Services (N = 7,693) are the top three industries that do not use promissory bills for payments. An investigation for such cross-industry differences might be an interesting future research topic.

We then interact the ratio of payment by promissory bills with other variables. This analysis is to examine the characteristics of firms that use promissory bills. When interacted with other variables, the ratio of promissory bills exhibits an inverted U-shape, as shown in Fig. 9 for the case when it is interacted with the number of employees (N = 147,590: cash only firms are excluded). A similar shape

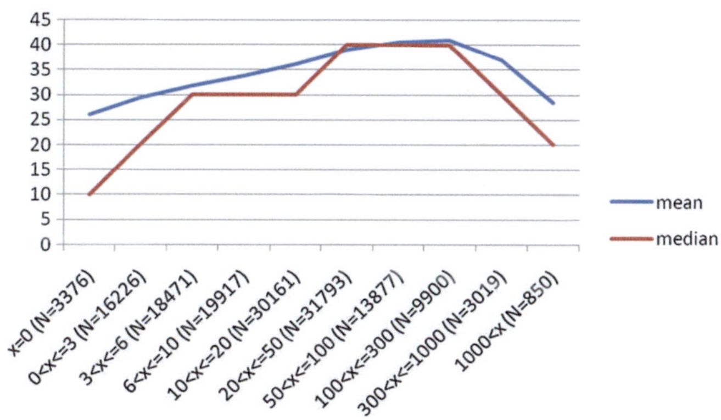

Fig. 9 Bill ratio (%) by firm size (x = # of employees) (excluding cash only firms)

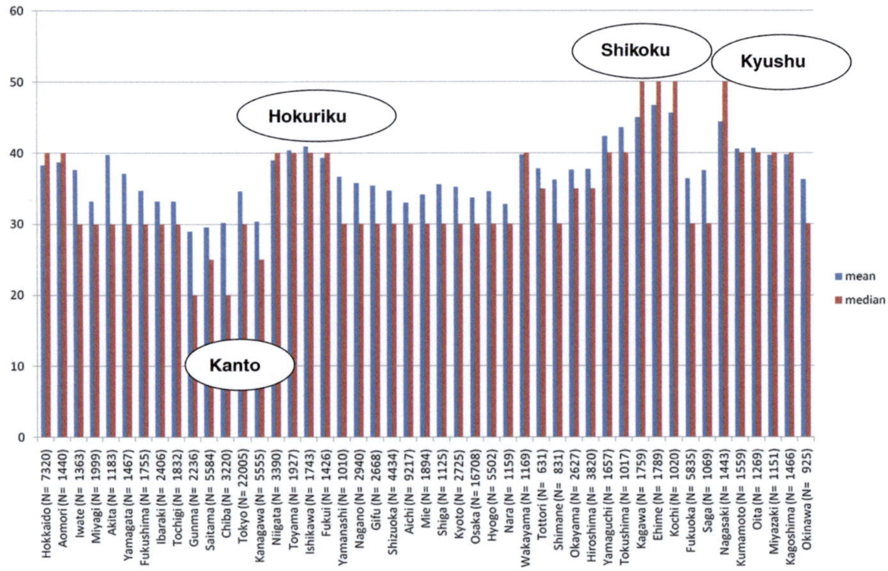

Fig. 10 Bill ratio (%) by prefecture (excluding cash only firms)

is observed when the cash ratio is interacted with the credit score (N = 147,466: firms rated between 60 and 65 use bills the most), capital asset ratio (N = 107,925: firms with 10–20 % use the most), capital stock (N = 107,455: firms with capital stock of 100–200 million yen use the most), operating revenue (N = 80,470: firms with operating revenue of 3–5 billion yen use the most), number of suppliers (N = 141,919: firms with 100–300 suppliers use the most), and the interest bearing debt to operating revenue ratio (N = 72,889: firms with ratio 8–10 use the most). These findings imply that promissory bills are used for payment by intermediate firms. However, when interacted with net current profit, the means and the medians are between 30 and 40 %, and no clear relationship exists.

The increasing part of the inverted U-shape indicates that a certain level of creditworthiness is needed for firms to be able to use promissory bills. The reason for this requirement might be because banks do not allow small firms to open a checking account. Because checking accounts are used to settle bills, such firms cannot use promissory bills. The decreasing part of the inverted U-shape might reflect the greater availability of alternative financing sources for more creditworthy firms.

We then proceed to the difference in the use of promissory bills by region. As shown in Fig. 10, we find some regional differences (excluding cash only firms, N = 148,270). In this figure, prefectures are sorted from north (left) to south (right). We find that firms in the Kanto area use bills less extensively, while those in Shikoku, Hokuriku, and Kyushu use more extensively. Some of these differences might reflect the difference in the composition of the industries. For example, prefectures in the southern Kanto area that include Chiba, Saitama, and Kanagawa have larger shares of non-manufacturing industries than other prefectures, which might well decrease the use of promissory bills. However, significant regional differences will probably remain even after controlling for the difference in the industry composition, which might be due to the differences in the degree of intra- versus inter-area transactions.

3.3.4 Univariate Analysis (3): Bill Endorsement

We already find in Table 19 that payment by endorsing promissory bills is not a common method of payment. Our findings are similar even when we break down the sample firms depending on their industry as in Fig. 11 (N = 148,105: cash only firms are excluded). As shown in this figure, the median ratio is zero for all of the industries. However, in means, endorsements account for more than 5 % of the payments for firms in Construction, Manufacturing, and Wholesale (Mining also, but the number of observation is small). Because these are the industries that also depend on promissory bills as a method of payment, our findings here imply that intra-industry trades that use new or discounted promissory bills are frequent in these industries. However, in these industries, there are only a small number of firms that use endorsement as a dominant method of payment.

Endorsement is used by smaller and less creditworthy firms. As Fig. 12 shows, the mean endorsement ratio decreases with the number of employees (N = 147,524). Similarly, it decreases with the credit score (N = 147,401), capital stock (N = 107,401), the interest bearing debt to operating revenue ratio (N = 141,603), and with the number of suppliers when these variables are large and does not increase when they are small. However, no clear relationship exists when the

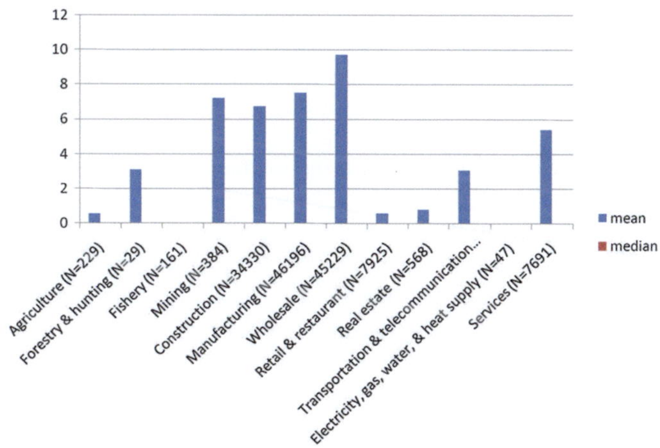

Fig. 11 Bill endorsement ratio (%) by industry (excluding cash only firms)

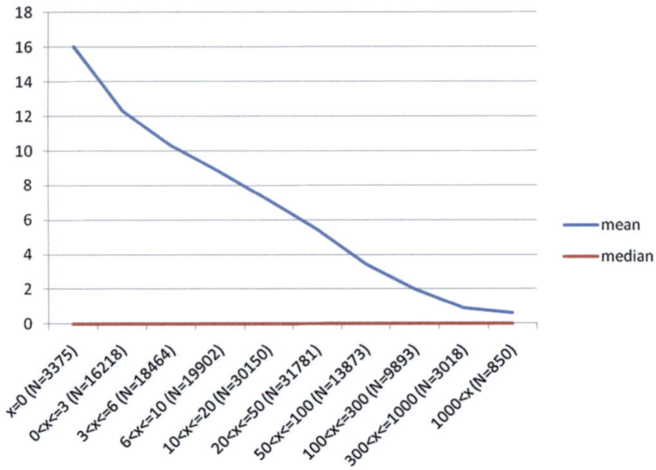

Fig. 12 Bill endorsement ratio (%) by firm size (x = # of employees) (excluding cash only firms)

endorsement ratio is interacted with the capital asset ratio and the net current profit. Also, the median ratio is always zero for all the categories of the base variables.

An interesting research question might be when or for what characteristics of firms do bill endorsements help to improve their financial conditions. Our findings here imply that less creditworthy firms, which might find it difficult to issue their own bills, rely on bill endorsement.

3.3.5 Univariate Analysis (4): Setting-Off

Similar to bill endorsement, setting-off is also a minor method of payment. Even if the sample firms are categorized by their industries (N = 148,076, cash only firms are excluded), the median ratios are always zero. However, we find that Agriculture (6.1 %), Fishery (4.3 %), and Manufacturing firms (4.0 %) use setting-off relatively frequently. The number of observations for the first two of these industries is small, however (Fig. 13).

When interacted with other variables, the median setting-off ratios are zero for all of the categories of the base variables. However, in terms of its mean, the ratio exhibits a rotated-S shape in the number of employees (N = 147,495) as shown in Fig. 14. This relationship might reflect the fact that, to use setting-off for payment, firms must have transactions of sufficient size. A similar, but less clear rotated-S shape is observed with respect to credit score (N = 147,372) and to capital stock (N = 107,383). The mean ratio exhibits a U-shape with respect to net current profit (N = 83,878), increases with the operating revenue (N = 80,412) and decreases with the interest bearing debt to operating revenue ratio (N = 72,836) and in the number of suppliers (N = 141,829). No clear relationship exists with respect to the capital asset ratio (N = 107,852).

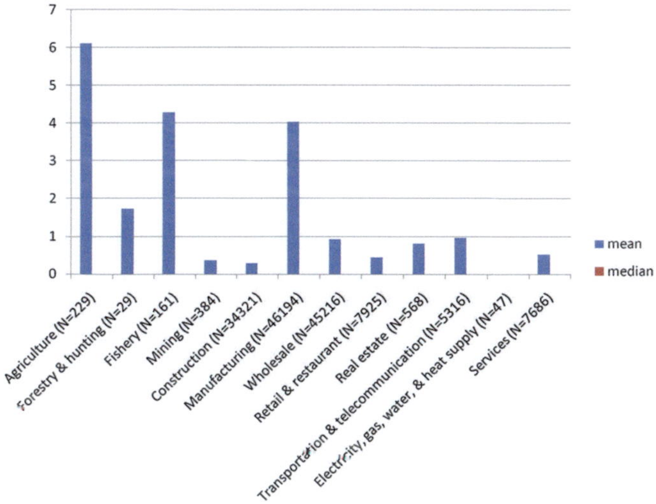

Fig. 13 Setting-off ratio (%) by industry (excluding cash only firms)

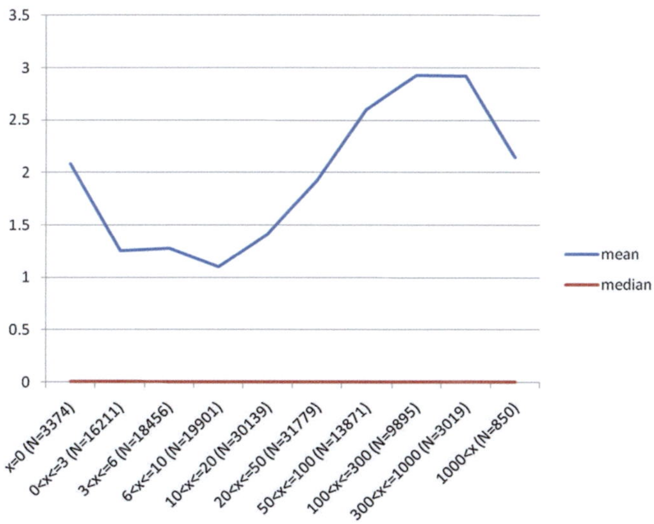

Fig. 14 Setting-off ratio (%) by firm size (x = # of employees) (excluding cash only firms)

3.3.6 Univariate Analysis (5): Prepayment

Finally, we consider the characteristics of firms that use prepayment. As show above, prepayment is also a minor method of payment. Consistent with this finding, the median prepayment ratio is zero for all the industries as shown in Fig. 15 (N = 148,059: cash only firms are excluded). However, as the mean figures show,

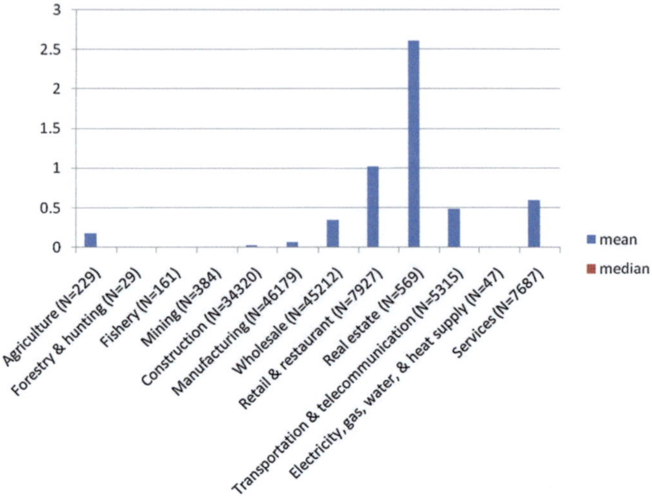

Fig. 15 Prepayment ratio (%) by industry (excluding cash only firms)

Real-estate firms (2.6 %) and Retail and restaurant firms (1.0 %) predominantly use prepayment. In these industries, payment in advance might be a convention.

When interacted with other variables, the mean fraction of prepayment decreases with the number of employees (N = 147,478), credit score (N = 147,355: Fig. 16), capital stock (N = 107,370), and the operating revenue (N = 80,403) at a decreasing rate. This decrease means that small and less creditworthy firms tend to use prepayment. The mean ratio also decreases with the capital asset ratio, except for those firms in the highest capital-asset-ratio category (i.e., 90–100 %, N = 107,839). However, because Real-estate firms tend to use prepayment frequently, these

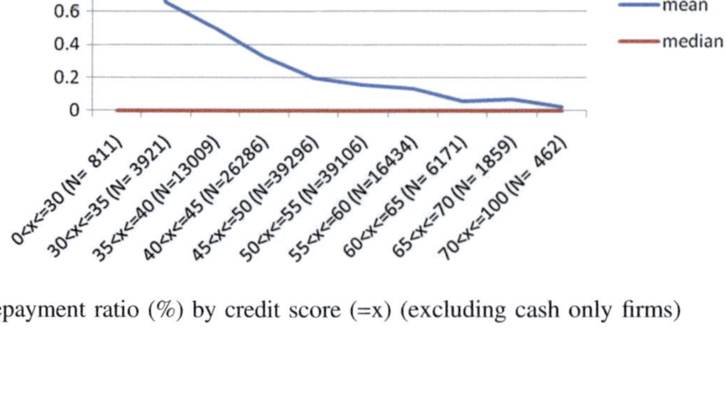

Fig. 16 Prepayment ratio (%) by credit score (=x) (excluding cash only firms)

findings might alternatively imply that Real-estate firms that use prepayment are small, less creditworthy, and have a high capital asset ratio. We find a less clear relationship between the prepayment ratio and net current profit, although the relationship looks like an inverted-U shape (N = 83,868). No clear relationship exists with respect to the interest bearing debt to operating revenue ratio (N = 72,827). The median prepayment ratios are zero for all of the categories broken down by these variables.

3.4 Method of Payment (for Firms as Payees)

3.4.1 Composition

In addition to information on the methods of payment that our sample firms use to *make* payments to their suppliers (as payers), the TDB also has information on the methods of payment that the same firms use to *receive* payments from their buyers (as payees). The information available is the fractions of payments received from the buyers in the form of (1) cash (including bank transfer, wire transfer, and checks), (2) promissory bills (including endorsed promissory bills), (3) setting-off (with trade payables), and/or (4) prepayment. In this subsection, we report our findings based on this payee information. In the analysis, we also report the results when we compare the methods of payment that the same firms use as payers and as payees.

When we first focus on the binary choice between using each of the methods to receive payment or not, we find that the fractions of firms that use each method (for any non-zero amount) are 99.48 % for cash (N = 368,898), 44.16 % for promissory bills (N = 368,745), 2.33 % for setting-off (N = 368,658), and 1.54 % for prepayment (N = 368,657). Similar to the methods to make payment as payers (Sect. 3.3.1), the most dominant method of payment that firms receive is cash. We find that 54.43 % of the firms accept cash only when they receive payments. This figure is slightly smaller than the ratio of firms that use cash only when they make payments as payers (59.74 %). The number of firms that never receive cash is 1,906 (0.52 %).

We also have information on the fraction of each method of payment that our sample firms receive to the total amount of payment they receive. Table 20 shows the summary statistics for the fraction. Similar to the case of the methods of payment used as payers (Sect. 3.3.1), the most dominant method of payment that firms receive as payees is cash. Also, the median firms never receive the other methods of payment. Compared with Table 19, the mean cash ratio (for receiving payment) in row (1) of this table (84.3 %) is slightly higher than the mean cash ratio (for making payment) (81.9 %: Table 19).

Promissory bills account for 14 % of the payments that our sample firms receive (in the mean). This fraction is comparable to the fraction of bills in the total payments (14.36 %: Table 19). However, it should be noted that receiving endorsed

Table 20 Fractions of methods used to receive payment

Method	N	Mean	SD	Min	p1	p50	p99	Max
(1) Cash	368,898	84.281	24.180	0	10	100	100	100
(2) Promissory bills	368,745	14.434	22.852	0	0	0	90	100
(3) Setting-off	368,658	0.557	4.844	0	0	0	20	100
(4) Precollection	368,657	0.711	7.137	0	0	0	20	100

bills are included in the figures in row (2) of this table, but writing out new bills and endorsing already issued ones are separate in rows (2) and (3) in Table 19 (where the mean ratio for payment by bill endorsement is 2.96 %). Among those firms that accept any amount of promissory bills for receiving payment from buyers, the bills are in general secondary methods of payment. If we exclude those firms that do not use the bills and categorize the remaining firms (N = 162,835) for each 5 % interval, more than half (59.7 %) of such firms accept promissory bills for less than 30 % of the payments they receive.

The other two methods of payment are rarely used to receive payments, as shown by a fraction of less than 1 %. We find that setting-off is a secondary method to receive payment, because even if we exclude firms that never accept setting-off (N = 8,605), it accounts for only 15 % or less of the total amount of payments that they receive for more than half of those firms. However, prepayment might be used as a dominant method of receiving payments. Although the prepayment ratio is less than 30 % for 54 % of the firms that use a non-zero percent of prepayment (N = 5,685), another 20 % of these firms accept prepayment only. The mean prepayment ratio (0.71 %) is higher than the mean prepayment ratio (0.10 %).

3.4.2 Univariate Analysis (1): Cash

As for the ratio of cash in the total amount of payments that our sample firms receive as payees, when we break it down by industry (N = 368,396: Fig. 17), the median ratio is 100 %, except for Mining (60 %), Construction (95 %), Manufacturing (70 %), and Wholesale (90 %). The mean ratios are lower, including these industries. In these respects, the cash ratio for receiving payments exhibits similar characteristics to the cash ratio for making payments (Sect. 3.3.2). In contrast, Retail and restaurant depend greatly on cash. As for Real-estate firms for which we found that the cash ratio for making payments was the highest (98.5 % in mean and 100 % in median), the cash ratio for receiving payments is smaller and is 92.0 %.

When decomposed by firm size (the number of employees) (N = 363,777), the mean cash ratio exhibits a U-shape, with firms that hire 20–50 employees receiving cash the least (but with 80.0 %) (see Fig. 18). A U-shaped relationship also exists when we interact the cash ratio with the capital asset ratio (N = 233,811), capital stock (N = 232,307), interest bearing debt to operating revenue ratio (N = 141,823), and the number of customers (N = 239,566). The categories for which the cash ratio

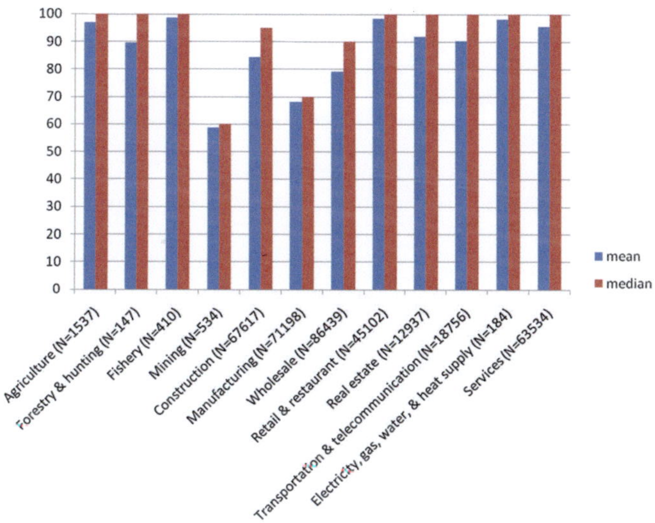

Fig. 17 Cash ratio (%) by industry

is the lowest are: 30–40 % of the capital asset ratio, 10–20 million yen of the capital stock, 5–8 of the interest bearing debt to operating revenue ratio, and 100–300 customers. As Fig. 18 shows, the shape of the median cash ratio is similar to that of the mean ratio.

As shown in Fig. 19, when we interact the cash ratio with the credit score (N = 363,258), we find that the ratio is lower for highly rated firms, although the highest-scored firms accept cash slightly more extensively (in the mean). A similar

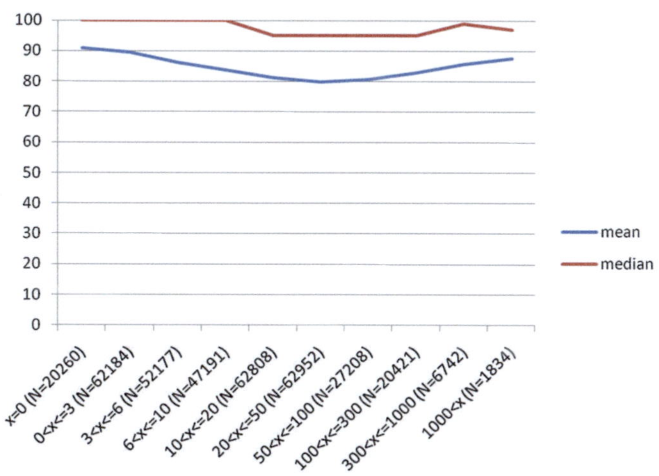

Fig. 18 Cash ratio (%) by firm size (x = the number of employees)

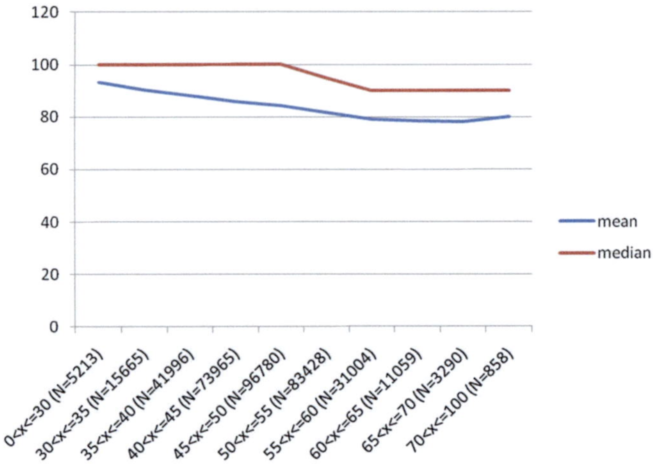

Fig. 19 Cash ratio (%) by credit score (=x)

relationship exists when the sample firms are categorized by operating revenue (N = 162,345). The cash ratio is the lowest for the credit score category of 65–70 and for the operating revenue category of 3–5 billion yen.

When categorized by the net current profit (N = 170,350), the mean cash ratio is W-shaped, that is, it is higher around the zero-profit, the highest (positive), and the lowest (negative) categories. However, the median ratio exhibits an inverted-V shape. Again, these characteristics of the cash ratio for payees are in general similar to those of the cash ratio as payers (Sect. 3.3.2).

When these two ratios, that is, the ratios of cash to make and receive payments, are interacted with each other, they have an increasing relationship (N = 364,968). With respect to the ratios for other methods of payment, the cash ratio of the firms as payees decreases with their promissory bill ratio (N = 364,853) and the bill endorsement ratio (N = 364,788) as payers, and does generally so with their setting-off ratio as payers (N = 364,758). Its mean also decreases with the prepayment ratio as payers (N = 364,743). These findings seem to indicate that the firms tend to make payments to their sellers using the same methods as the ones that they use to receive payments from their customers.

However, other findings suggest that cash is a dominant method when firms receive payments. First, even when the firms use other methods to make payments, the cash ratio for receiving payments is high (e.g., the median cash ratio for payees is 75 % for 100 % bill payment firms and is 30 % for 100 % setting-off payment firms). Also, the median is 100 % for most of the categories broken down by the prepayment ratio for making payments.

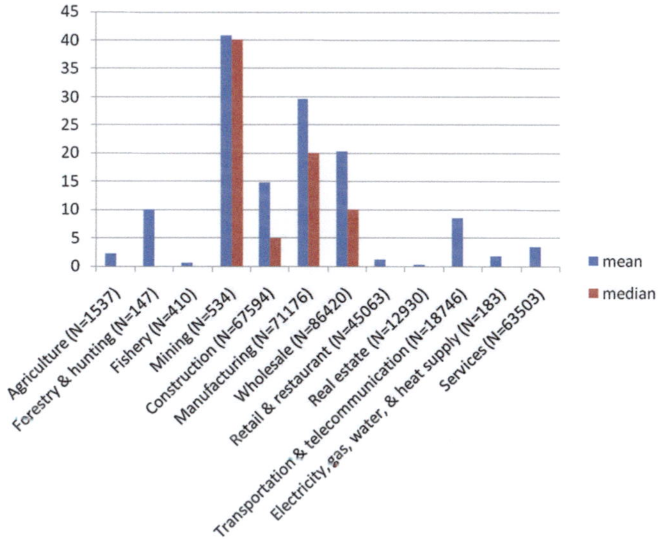

Fig. 20 Bill ratio (%) by industry

3.4.3 Univariate Analysis (2): Promissory Bills

Turning to the difference in the use of promissory bills as a method to receive payments, as the medians in Fig. 20 show (N = 368,244), they are extensively used in Mining (40 %), Manufacturing (20 %), Wholesale (10 %), and Construction (5 %). For these four industries, the median bill ratio for receiving payments is greater than the median bill ratio for making payments, so firms in these industries collect more bills than they use. As the means in Fig. 20 indicate, Forestry and hunting (10.0 %) and Transportation and telecommunication (8.5 %) also accept promissory bills to some extent, although the number of observations for Forestry and hunting is small.

Figure 21 shows the mean and the median bill ratio when we exclude firms that accept cash only (N = 168,882). In Sect. 3.3.3, we show that the mean and median of the ratios of promissory bills to make payments are around 20–40 % for each industry when we exclude cash only firms. The mean and the median bill ratios (for receiving payments) shown in this figure are thus smaller than the corresponding ratios in Sect. 3.3.3 in most industries, which indicates that when they are used, promissory bills are more frequently used as a method to make payments than as a method to receive payments. However, the numbers of excluded firms (i.e., cash only firms) differ in these two cases.

The ratio of promissory bills for receiving payments has an inverted U-shape when interacted with the number of employees (Fig. 22: cash only firms are excluded, N = 168,099). Promissory bills are most extensively accepted by middle-sized firms with 20–50 employees. A similar inverted U-shape is observed when the

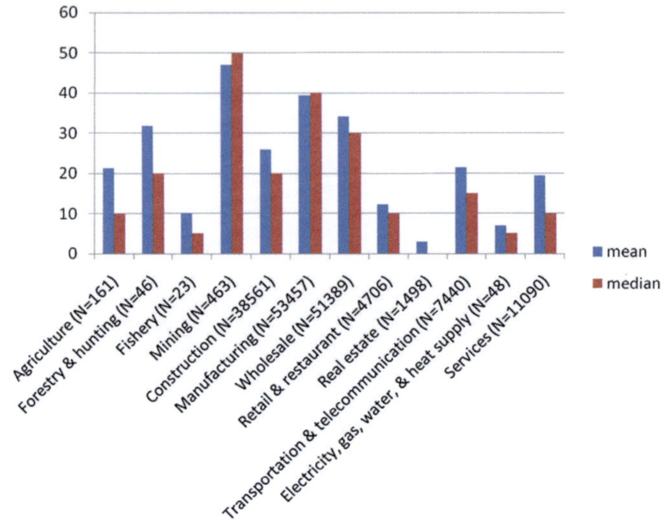

Fig. 21 Bill ratio (%) by industry (excluding cash only firms)

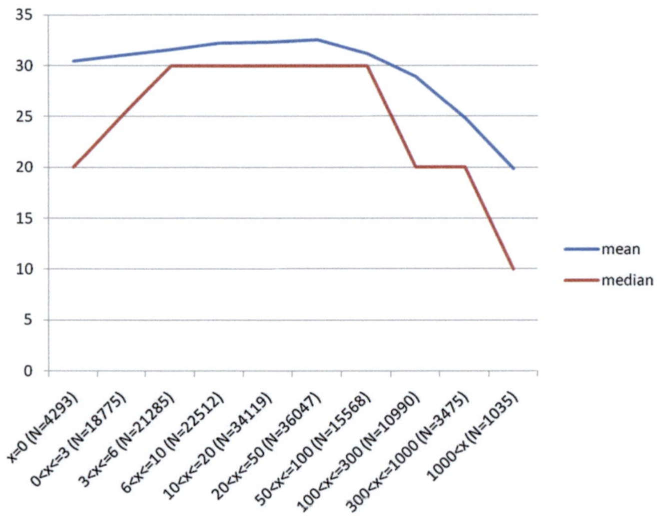

Fig. 22 Bill ratio (%) by firm size (x = # of employees) (excluding cash only firms)

ratio is interacted with the credit score (N = 167,921: firms rated between 40 and 45 use bills the most), capital asset ratio (N = 123,320: firms with 10–20 % use the most), capital stock (N = 122,795: firms with capital stock of 5–10 million yen use the most), operating revenue (N = 91,932: firms with operating revenue of 3–5 billion yen use the most), and the interest bearing debt to operating revenue ratio (N = 82,899: firms with ratio 5–8 use the most). When interacted with the net

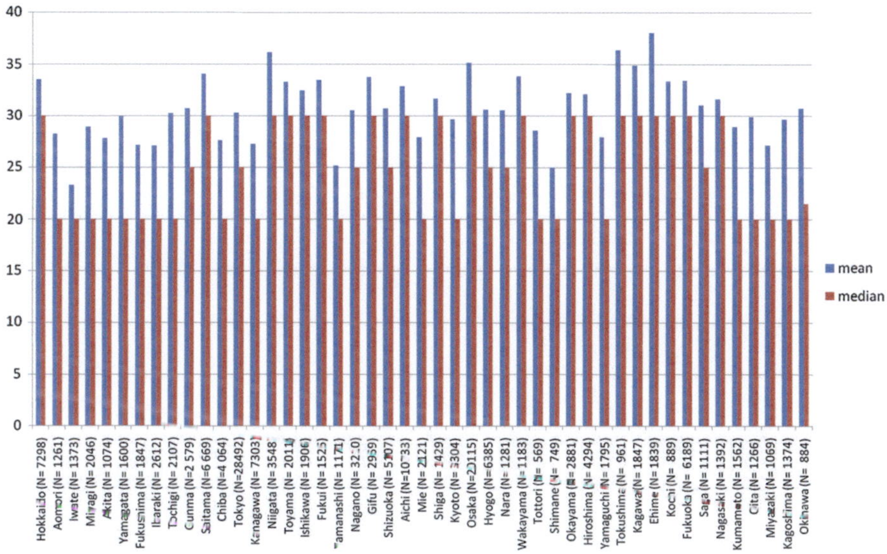

Fig. 23 Bill ratio (%) by prefecture (excluding cash only firms)

current profit, the means and the medians are between 20–30 %, and no clear relationship exists. These characteristics are similar to those we observed with respect to the bill ratio for payers (Sect. 3.3.3).

Compared with the bill ratio for payers by prefecture (Fig. 10), we see less dispersion and smaller levels for the means and medians of the bill ratio for payees across prefectures (Fig. 23: N = 168,985). In Fig. 10, we find that promissory bills are extensively used to make payments in the Hokuriku, Shikoku, and Kyushu areas and less extensively in the Kanto area. Similar tendencies also exist in this figure, but less clearly.

The bill ratio for the firms as payees decreases with their cash ratio (N = 168,075), setting-off ratio (N = 167,934), and prepayment ratio (N = 167,916) as payers, but increases with their bill ratio (N = 168,011) and bill endorsement ratio (N = 167,964) as payers. These relationships again suggest a correlation between the methods of making and receiving payments.

As a final analysis on promissory bills, we decompose the sample firms depending on whether the firms have their banks discount any bills or not. For those firms that have their banks discount bills, the promissory bill ratio (for payees) is on average 44.1 % (in mean) or 40 % (in median) of the total payment, whereas for those that do not have their bank discount promissory bills, the ratio is 13.3 % (in the mean) or zero (in the median). These findings indicate that firms that extensively accept promissory bills as a method of payment are more likely to have the bills discounted by banks.

Consistent with these findings, we also find that the mean and the median bill ratios increase with the *amount* of bills discounted by banks. This increase means

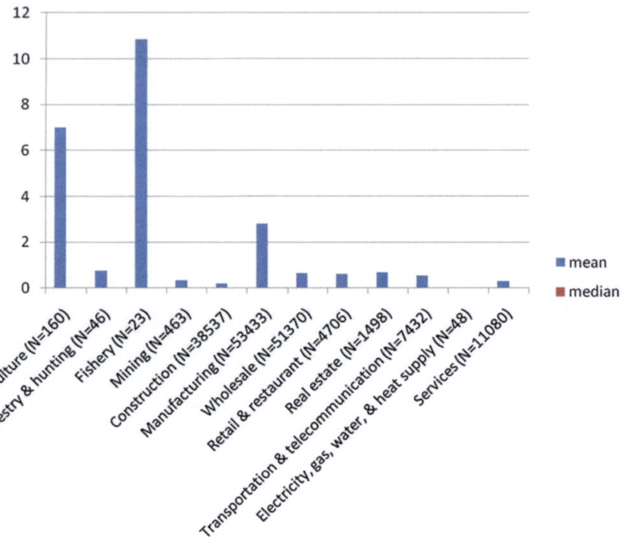

Fig. 24 Setting-off ratio (%) by industry (excluding cash only firms)

that those firms that accept more promissory bills have their banks discount them more extensively. However, this finding is based on a small number of observations for this decomposition (N = 57,167).

3.4.4 Univariate Analysis (3): Setting-Off

Turning to the payments received using the setting-off, when we calculate the mean and the median of the setting-off ratio by industry (N = 168,796), the medians are zero for all of the industries, which implies that the setting-off is never extensively accepted in any industries. In the means, however, Fishery (10.9 %), Agriculture (7.0 %), and Manufacturing (2.8 %) firms receive relatively more setting-off. In Sect. 3.3.5, we show that these are also industries that use the setting-off for making payments. However, the first two of these industries have very few observations (Fig. 24).

When interacted with other variables, the medians for the setting-off ratio (for payees) are zero for all of the categories. As Fig. 25 shows with respect to firm size (N = 168,013: cash only firms are excluded), the mean ratios exhibit a rotated-S shapc as in the case of the setting-off ratio for payers (Sect. 3.3.5). Similarly, we find a less clear, rotated-S shape with respect to the credit score (N = 167,837: no cash only firms) and the capital stock (N = 122,733: no cash only firms). The mean setting-off ratio exhibits a U-shape with respect to the net current profit (N = 95,615: no cash only firms); increases with the operating revenue (N = 87,486: no cash only firms); and decreases with the capital asset ratio (N = 123,257: no cash only firms), the interest bearing debt to operating revenue ratio (N = 82,864: no cash only firms), and with the number of suppliers (N = 142,688: no cash only firms).

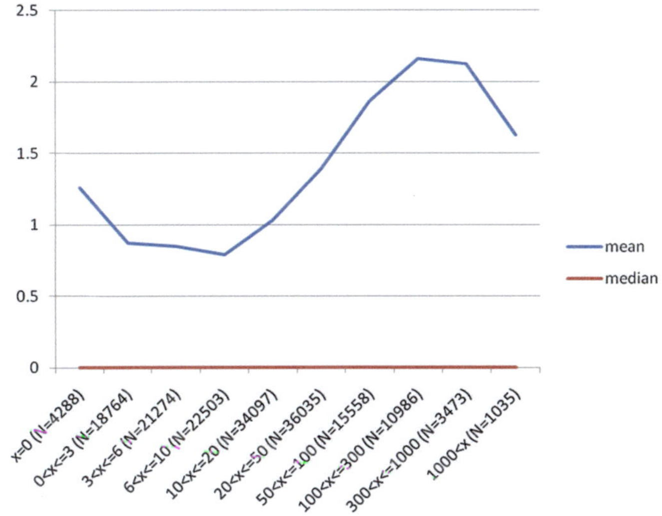

Fig. 25 Setting-off ratio (%) by firm size (x = # of employees) (excluding cash only firms)

An interesting exercise is to compare the firms' ratio of setting-off in receiving payments with the ratios of their other methods of making payments. We find that the mean setting-off ratio (for receiving payments) decreases with the ratio of cash payments (N = 167,993: no cash only firms) at a decreasing rate, and generally decreases with the ratios of payments by promissory bills (N = 167,929: no cash only firms) and by bill endorsement (N = 167,885: no cash only firms). However, the mean setting-off ratio for receiving payments increases with the setting-off ratio for making payments (Fig. 26: N = 167,855: no cash only firms). No clear relationship exists with respect to the prepayment ratio (N = 167,837: no cash only firms). These findings imply that only firms that extensively use the setting-off for payment receive setting-off.

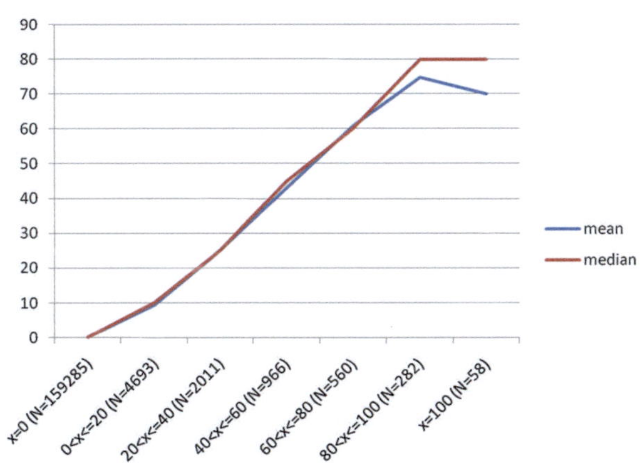

Fig. 26 Setting-off ratios for firms as payees and as payers (as payers = x) (excluding cash only firms)

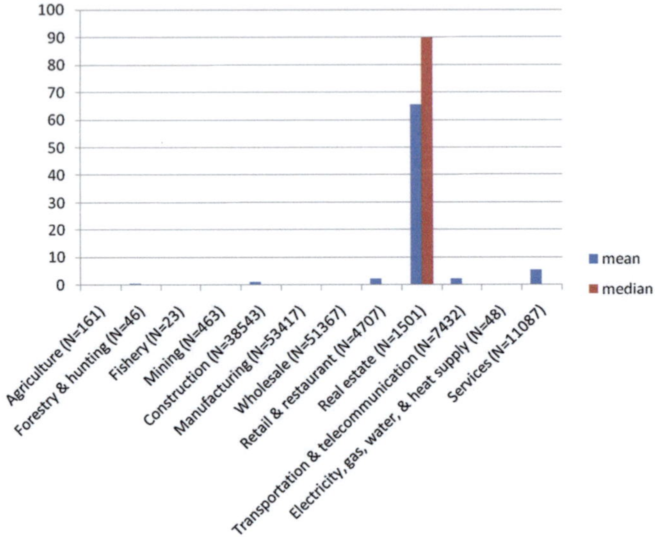

Fig. 27 Prepayment ratio (%) by industry (excluding cash only firms)

3.4.5 Univariate Analysis (4): Prepayment

When broken down by industry (N = 168,795: cash only firms are excluded), we find that the prepayment is clearly used by Real-estate firms (Fig. 27). More than half of the Real-estate firms use prepayment for 90 % of the payments that they receive from their customers (when they do not receive cash). We observed earlier that Real-estate firms use prepayment to make payments relatively frequently, but its mean and median were respectively 2.6 % and zero (Sect. 3.3.6). This finding together with the finding in Fig. 27 means that prepayment is not necessarily simultaneously used for making and receiving payments. A possible reason for this asymmetry is that Real-estate firms pay to firms, but receive payments from retail customers.

Even eliminating those firms that receive payment in cash only, the median prepayment ratio is zero for all of the categories with the base variables. In terms of its mean, the ratio decreases at a decreasing rate with the number of employees (N = 168,012), credit score (N = 167,836: shown in Fig. 28), operating revenue (N = 91,892), and the number of customers (N = 142,676). These findings imply that small and less creditworthy firms tend to use prepayment. The mean ratio is U-shaped with respect to the capital asset ratio (N = 123,260) and is less clearly so with respect to the interest bearing debt to operating revenue ratio (N = 82,867). No clear relationship exists when interacted with the capital stock and the net current profit.

When interacted with the cash ratio for making payments (N = 167,992: excluding those firms that receive cash only), the mean prepayment ratio for

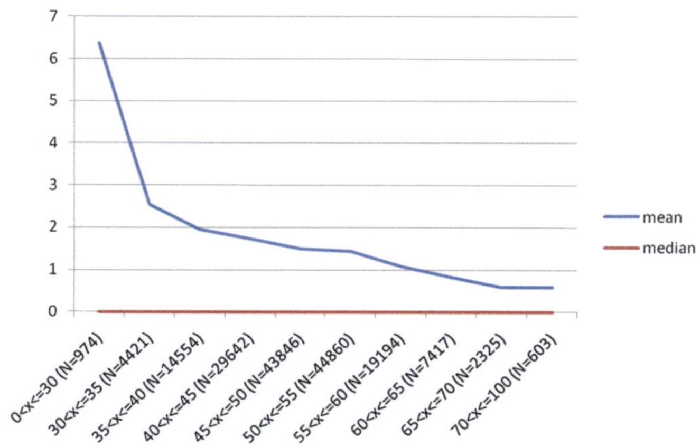

Fig. 28 Prepayment ratio (%) by credit score (=x) (excluding cash only firms)

receiving payments is the highest (4.73 %) for firms paying with 100 % cash (N = 44,952). Interestingly, firms that never pay by cash also use prepayment for receiving payments relatively extensively (5.9 %), although the number of observations is small (N = 467). The mean prepayment ratio is less than 1 % for the other intermediate categories.

With respect to other methods of making payments, the ratio of prepayment for receiving payments is relatively higher for firms using no promissory bills (3.3 % of N = 167,928 (excluding cash only firms)), no bill endorsement (1.9 % of N = 167,885 (excluding cash only firms)), or no setting-off (1.6 % of N = 167,855 (excluding cash only firms)) for making payment. However, the means for the other categories (broken down by the bill ratio, the bill endorsement ratio, or the setting-off ratio for making payment) are all less than 0.5 %, and the median is zero for all the categories. Finally, the prepayment ratio for firms as payees increases with the prepayment ratio for them as payers (N = 167,836) at an increasing rate (Fig. 29), although the majority of our sample firms never use prepayment for making or receiving payments.

3.5 Trade Credit Days

3.5.1 Closing Day

As explained in Sect. 3.2 (Fig. 3), there are several important days for processing trade credit. In this subsection, we present the statistics for these days. This overview also helps us to grasp the length of the credit period, which will be focused on in the next section (Sect. 3.6).

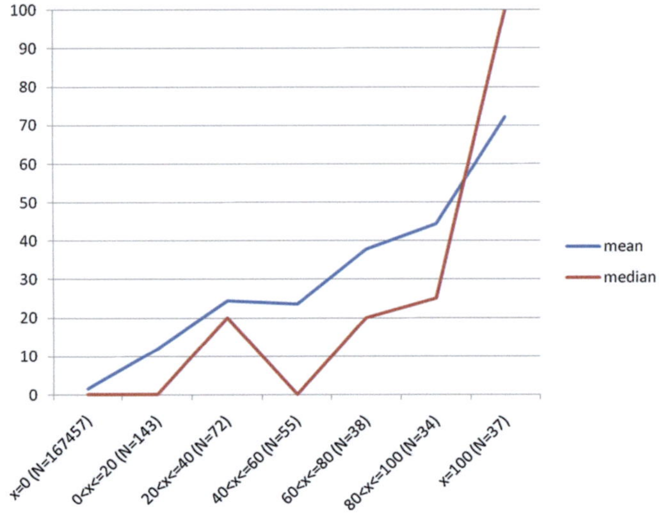

Fig. 29 Prepayment ratios for firms as payees and as payers (%) (as payers = x) (excluding cash only firms)

First, with respect to a closing day, two different pieces of information are available from the TDB: closing days for the firms' *primary* method of payment and for their *secondary* one (if any). The data show that almost all of the sample firms have a closing day: 99.84 % of them have a closing day for their primary method of payment (N = 337,868) and 99.60 % have one for their secondary method of payment (N = 46,290).

For reference, a survey conducted in 2008 by the Research Institute of Economy, Trade, and Industry reported a smaller percentage (90.3 %) of sample firms with a closing day (see Uesugi et al. 2009).[14] The major difference between our sample firms and those in this survey is that the survey asks the responding firms about the primary payment methods that they use with respect to their *main* suppliers only. The difference might also stem from the smaller sample size of the firms as compared with our large number of firms.

We also find that the closing day is almost always set within the same month as when the transaction was made. The number of firms that set it in a different month (e.g., in the next month) is only 16 (out of 337,184 firms) for the primary payment and 24 (out of 472,662 firms) for the secondary payment. These exceptions are not specific to a particular region or industry.

As shown in Table 21, the majority of firms (68.2 %) set a closing day on the 31st (end of month) of each month, while many others set one on the 20th (26.39 %) (for the primary payment method). The dates other than these two are relatively infrequent. Among them, the 25th (2.24 %) and the 15th (2.02 %) are the

[14] The sample firms are about 5,700 firms that are mostly small- and medium-sized enterprises.

Table 21 Date of the monthly closing day

Primary payment method			Secondary payment method		
Date in a month	Freq.	Percentage	Date in a month	Freq.	Percentage
5th	427	0.13	5	102	0.22
10th	2,576	0.76	10	548	1.19
15th	6,808	2.02	15	1,684	3.66
20th	88,928	26.39	20	12,493	27.14
25th	7,566	2.24	25	1,268	2.76
30th	632	0.19	30	140	0.30
31st	229,790	68.18	31	29,700	64.53
Others	306	0.09	Others	89	0.20
Total	337,033	100	Total	46,024	100

next most used, followed by the 10th (0.76 %), the 30th (0.19 %), and the 5th (0.13 %). Similar relationships exist with respect to the firms' secondary payment method, although the distribution is slightly more dispersed.

Table 22 shows the distribution of the closing day's date in a month for the primary payment method depending on the firms' prefecture (N = 337,037). The firms in southern Japan (those in Kyushu Island (Fukuoka, Saga, Nagasaki, Kumamoto, Oita, Miyazaki, and Kagoshima and Okinawa) have a tendency to set a closing day at the end of the month, while those in central Japan [especially those in the Hokuriku region (Toyama, Ishikawa, Fukui)] frequently set a closing day on the 20th. We find similar, but less clear, regional differences for a closing day for the secondary payment method. In Sect. 3.3.3, we show similar regional differences in the use of promissory bills. These findings might indicate that commercial transactions in these areas, Kyushu and Hokuriku, are respectively clustered. It might be interesting to investigate whether, and how, this pattern reflects historical background as well.

There is also some industry specificity in the distribution of the closing day's date in a month (Table 23: N = 336,621). The firms in primary industries, for example, Transportation and telecommunication and Services firms, have a higher tendency to set a closing day at the month's end, while the 20th is relatively common for firms in Wholesale and Manufacturing industries.

3.5.2 Payment Day

Similar to a closing day, two different pieces of information about a payment day are available: the payment day for the firms' *primary* method of payment and for their *secondary* one (if any). From the TDB data, we find that a payment day is usually set in the month next to the one when the deal is done [for 83.38 % of the sample firms (N = 337,322)]. However, a non-negligible fraction of firms set the

Table 22 Closing day's date (=x) by prefecture (primary payment method)

Pref.	x = 5th (%)	x = 10th (%)	x = 15th (%)	x = 20th (%)	x = 25th (%)	x = 31st (%)	Others (%)	Total (%)
Hokkaido	0.09	0.44	0.85	26.17	1.92	70.41	0.12	100
Aomori	0.11	0.36	1.39	23.32	1.61	73.14	0.07	100
Iwate	0.15	0.49	0.65	17.43	2.02	79.03	0.23	100
Miyagi	0.15	0.67	1.11	16.36	1.94	79.67	0.10	100
Akita	0.00	0.51	1.80	25.96	2.14	69.20	0.39	100
Yamagata	0.24	0.68	1.32	26.62	2.04	68.87	0.23	100
Fukushima	0.05	0.34	0.80	16.27	2.06	80.33	0.15	100
Ibaraki	0.21	0.68	1.41	17.54	2.09	77.97	0.10	100
Tochigi	0.15	0.76	1.11	17.88	2.64	77.26	0.20	100
Gunma	0.16	0.82	1.47	25.07	3.90	68.38	0.20	100
Saitama	0.16	0.94	1.77	23.81	2.60	70.53	0.19	100
Chiba	0.13	1.03	1.85	20.61	2.38	73.91	0.09	100
Tokyo	0.17	1.00	2.12	21.35	1.44	73.47	0.45	100
Kanagawa	0.11	0.70	1.66	17.73	2.35	76.88	0.57	100
Niigata	0.07	0.67	2.07	**45.95**	3.90	**47.17**	0.17	100
Toyama	0.07	0.66	1.56	**50.35**	3.15	**44.11**	0.10	100
Ishikawa	0.06	0.28	1.52	**46.34**	4.28	**47.34**	0.18	100
Fukui	0.00	0.61	1.67	**51.45**	7.62	**38.44**	0.21	100
Yamanashi	0.04	0.50	1.40	18.94	4.75	74.21	0.16	100
Nagano	0.13	0.84	1.30	29.78	3.12	64.56	0.27	100

(continued)

Table 22 (continued)

Pref.	x = 5th (%)	x = 10th (%)	x = 15th (%)	x = 20th (%)	x = 25th (%)	x = 31st (%)	Others (%)	Total (%)
Gifu	0.06	0.59	1.78	**43.92**	4.30	**49.15**	0.20	100
Shizuoka	0.08	0.52	1.17	22.92	3.59	71.61	0.11	100
Aichi	0.13	0.76	1.81	31.03	1.94	64.19	0.14	100
Mie	0.11	1.13	2.48	34.82	2.93	58.43	0.10	100
Shiga	0.08	0.61	3.37	**50.57**	1.83	**43.43**	0.11	100
Kyoto	0.09	0.95	4.02	**47.43**	2.25	**45.05**	0.21	100
Osaka	0.17	1.10	4.78	**41.68**	1.28	50.55	0.44	100
Hyogo	0.11	0.82	2.52	38.89	2.15	55.21	0.30	100
Nara	0.04	0.41	2.77	**44.50**	1.86	50.33	0.09	100
Wakayama	0.00	0.60	1.29	**43.13**	4.74	**49.70**	0.54	100
Tottori	0.17	0.86	2.84	34.17	3.36	58.35	0.25	100
Shimane	0.07	0.79	1.12	**41.41**	3.42	53.00	0.19	100
Okayama	0.10	0.39	1.39	18.97	4.10	74.99	0.06	100
Hiroshima	0.08	0.52	1.44	20.12	3.40	74.34	0.10	100
Yamaguchi	0.00	0.25	0.95	14.88	2.47	81.41	0.04	100
Tokushima	0.16	0.47	1.41	21.48	3.92	72.09	0.47	100
Kagawa	0.24	0.42	1.78	28.15	5.61	63.69	0.11	100
Ehime	0.09	0.35	0.92	20.22	4.14	74.09	0.19	100
Kochi	0.11	0.54	0.81	17.99	2.76	76.86	0.93	100
Fukuoka	0.05	0.63	1.14	12.87	1.53	83.60	0.18	100

(continued)

Table 22 (continued)

Pref.	x = 5th (%)	x = 10th (%)	x = 15th (%)	x = 20th (%)	x = 25th (%)	x = 31st (%)	Others (%)	Total (%)
Saga	0.16	0.52	1.09	12.86	1.82	83.56	0.00	100
Nagasaki	0.07	0.24	1.11	**9.97**	2.29	86.15	0.17	100
Kumamoto	0.08	0.46	1.09	13.31	2.01	82.91	0.14	100
Oita	0.07	0.22	0.85	10.91	1.74	86.16	0.05	100
Miyazaki	0.07	0.33	1.26	**9.67**	1.26	87.11	0.30	100
Kagoshima	0.09	0.34	0.71	**8.28**	1.24	89.30	0.04	100
Okinawa	0.04	0.32	0.64	**3.50**	0.67	94.49	0.34	100

Table 23 Closing day's date (=x) by industry (primary payment method)

Industry	x = 5th (%)	x = 10th (%)	x = 15th (%)	x = 20th (%)	x = 25th (%)	x = 31st (%)	Others (%)	Total (%)
Agriculture	0.00	0.53	0.83	6.70	1.20	**90.52**	0.23	100
Forestry and hunting	0.00	0.00	1.75	6.14	0.88	**91.23**	0.00	100
Fishery	0.00	0.00	0.00	5.42	1.81	**92.47**	0.30	100
Mining	0.00	0.20	0.20	13.32	2.98	**83.30**	0.00	100
Construction	0.28	1.37	2.14	**28.27**	4.41	63.30	0.22	100
Manufacturing	0.10	0.57	2.22	**30.98**	2.81	63.08	0.24	100
Wholesale	0.11	0.85	2.79	**35.83**	1.52	58.66	0.25	100
Retail and restaurant	0.07	0.50	1.97	**20.55**	1.09	75.52	0.29	100
Real estate	0.18	1.07	1.63	**20.92**	2.76	72.74	0.70	100
Transport. and telecom.	0.03	0.33	0.70	13.89	0.92	**83.88**	0.24	100
Electr., gas, water, and heat sup.	0.00	0.00	0.00	**21.02**	2.84	75.57	0.57	100
Services	0.07	0.49	1.09	15.36	1.36	**81.29**	0.34	100

payment day two months later (13.65 %). The corresponding figures in the case of the secondary method are respectively 65.47 % (next month) and 27.81 % (two months later).

When we break down the sample firms by their location, we find that the ratio of firms that set a payment day 2 months later is higher in eastern Japan, especially in the Kanto area (more than 15 % in the case of the primary method); while the ratio of the firms that set one in the next month is higher in western Japan. These regional differences overlap with those of the closing day. The prefectures with more firms setting a closing day on the 20th tend to have more firms with a payment day 2 months later, while those with more firms setting a closing day on the 31st have more firms with a payment day in the next month. For the secondary payment method, the later payment month for eastern prefectures is more clearly observed (for many prefectures 2 months later account for more than 35 %), but the earlier payment month for western prefectures is less clear.

When we break down the sample by industry (N = 336,928), the fraction of firms setting a payment day for the primary payment method in the next month is the highest in Forestry and hunting (90.5 %: N = 116), Retail and restaurant (90.4 %: N = 40,576), and Fishery (89.5 %: N = 332) firms, while setting 2 months later is highest in Transportation and telecommunication (22.7 %: N = 17,344), Services (19.2 %: N = 57,210), and Construction (16.8 %: N = 62,059) firms. As for the secondary payment method, the differences in the corresponding fractions by industry are less clear.

Within a month, a majority of firms set the payment day on the 31st (end of month) as shown in Table 24. However, the 10th and 20th are also common. Together with the finding above, the most common practice for credit payment for the firms in Japan is to *close at the end of the same month and pay at the end of the next month*; although, alternatively, the payment day might frequently be set on the 10th and 15th, and 2 months later.

Table 24 Date of the monthly payment day

Primary payment method			Secondary payment method		
Date in a month	Freq.	Percentage	Date in a month	Freq.	Percentage
5	15,218	4.53	5	2,554	5.28
10	46,612	13.86	10	6,985	14.45
15	27,274	8.11	15	5,310	10.98
20	43,941	13.07	20	6,680	13.82
25	18,928	5.63	25	2,599	5.38
30	1,018	0.3	30	402	0.83
31	176,704	52.55	31	22,594	46.73
Others	6,571	1.95	Others	1,224	2.53
Total	336,266	100	Total	48,348	100

Is there any regional difference in the distribution of a payment day within a month? We find some, as shown in Table 25, for the primary payment method (N = 336,294). A payment day on the 31st is more common for firms in Tohoku (northeastern, especially Iwate and Miyagi), Kanto (eastern, especially Ibaraki, Tokyo and Kanagawa), Kyushu (western, Fukuoka through Kagoshima), and Okinawa; whereas many firms set one on the 10th or the 20th in Hokuriku (north-central: Toyama, Ishikawa, and Fukui). As for the secondary payment method, we find less clear regional differences

Finally, we check whether the payment day differs by industry (Table 26: N = 335,879). Similar to the case of a closing day, we find that each month's end is most commonly set as the payment day for primary and tertiary industries (except for Retail and restaurant), and the 10th and 20th are frequently used by the secondary industries (and Wholesale). Again, such relationships are less clear in the case of a payment day for the secondary payment method.

On balance, we find interesting differences in the setting of a closing day and a payment day depending on the firms' location and industry. Some of the differences seem to link with each other because the differences exist between similar sets of prefectures and industries. However, the grouping of prefectures and industries does not necessarily overlap. It might be interesting to further pursue the interrelation between a closing day and a payment day and their regional and industry differences, not only from a theoretical but also from a historical perspective.

3.6 Credit Period

3.6.1 Length of Payment Period (Contracted Term)

We have different pieces of information about the credit period, that is, the duration for which sellers grant credit to buyers. In our case, the credit period is the payment period because we use information from the borrowers' viewpoint.

First, we can compute the lag (days) between a payment day and a closing day that we have already observed in the previous section. We label the number of days calculated in this manner as CP_DIFFERENCE. As we explained in Sect. 3.2, the invoice for a particular payment is processed on the buyer firm's closing day that comes after the deal. Also, the payment is made on the payment day that is after the closing day. So, if a deal is done on the closing day, the buyer receives an invoice immediately. And if the method of payment is cash in this case, the CP_DIFFERENCE equals the credit period. However, if a deal is done one day after the closing day of the buyer firm, for example, even if the payment is made by cash, the credit period is larger than CP_DIFFERENCE by 30 days (1 month), because the deal is processed on the next closing day.

Also, credit periods differ when promissory bills are used for the payment method. In this case, a payment day is the day that the seller receives a bill, not cash. Thus, the credit period is longer by the maturity of the promissory bill.

Table 25 Payment day's date (=x) by prefecture (primary payment method)

Pref.	x = 5th (%)	x = 10th (%)	x = 15th (%)	x = 20th (%)	x = 25th (%)	x = 31st (%)	Others (%)	Total (%)
Hokkaido	3.96	11.96	6.55	12.97	6.06	57.05	1.46	100
Aomori	4.07	13.48	8.50	12.16	4.98	54.73	2.10	100
Iwate	3.97	10.15	5.84	8.66	4.66	**64.92**	1.79	100
Miyagi	3.73	9.87	5.48	9.19	4.00	**66.05**	1.67	100
Akita	5.51	14.43	8.20	11.40	6.02	52.39	2.04	100
Yamagata	4.66	12.15	8.76	13.27	6.29	50.68	4.19	100
Fukushima	4.92	11.54	5.72	9.93	6.06	59.63	2.18	100
Ibaraki	4.53	12.40	5.77	10.47	4.71	**60.43**	1.69	100
Tochigi	5.38	11.64	8.29	11.20	5.92	55.29	2.30	100
Gunma	5.34	13.18	7.40	13.26	6.59	51.54	2.67	100
Saitama	6.68	13.02	7.09	11.24	5.32	54.77	1.88	100
Chiba	5.69	13.08	7.28	10.50	4.91	56.92	1.62	100
Tokyo	5.23	11.95	6.92	8.96	3.92	**61.11**	1.91	100
Kanagawa	6.13	11.95	7.01	8.51	3.77	**60.68**	1.96	100
Niigata	3.43	**20.50**	12.15	18.74	6.20	35.37	3.61	100
Toyama	2.92	19.84	12.82	**24.50**	7.40	30.58	1.94	100
Ishikawa	1.73	19.83	12.42	**26.64**	8.67	28.75	1.95	100
Fukui	2.53	**26.64**	17.86	**24.19**	6.58	20.80	1.38	100
Yamanashi	4.48	12.41	6.85	12.83	7.89	53.55	2.01	100
Nagano	4.16	15.13	8.51	15.42	7.75	45.64	3.39	100

(continued)

Table 25 (continued)

Pref.	x = 5th (%)	x = 10th (%)	x = 15th (%)	x = 20th (%)	x = 25th (%)	x = 31st (%)	Others (%)	Total (%)
Gifu	3.20	**20.32**	11.78	**20.38**	7.61	33.54	3.15	100
Shizuoka	4.25	13.03	7.33	14.29	8.10	50.42	2.57	100
Aichi	4.31	13.57	8.02	17.41	7.15	47.31	2.24	100
Mie	3.40	**20.53**	10.42	16.60	7.05	39.59	2.41	100
Shiga	4.06	**22.87**	12.02	**20.15**	4.83	34.16	1.90	100
Kyoto	5.82	**23.06**	11.22	16.23	5.78	36.02	1.88	100
Osaka	4.97	16.75	10.61	17.65	5.61	42.04	2.38	100
Hyogo	3.76	18.99	11.18	17.38	5.71	40.86	2.13	100
Nara	3.86	**21.00**	10.83	**20.71**	5.77	35.85	1.99	100
Wakayama	1.79	**24.87**	12.41	**21.29**	6.76	29.75	3.13	100
Tottori	3.03	15.14	11.59	16.87	7.79	40.57	5.02	100
Shimane	2.59	17.51	14.72	19.03	6.10	34.95	5.12	100
Okayama	3.21	14.20	7.23	15.10	8.94	48.11	3.21	100
Hiroshima	3.29	12.38	8.40	14.29	8.26	51.36	2.02	100
Yamaguchi	3.78	11.35	5.88	10.27	6.07	**60.55**	2.09	100
Tokushima	2.88	12.59	8.50	17.09	6.50	48.66	3.77	100
Kagawa	3.08	17.72	10.79	16.53	10.12	37.90	3.87	100
Ehime	2.42	13.27	9.20	13.65	7.16	51.00	3.32	100
Kochi	2.71	14.58	8.24	13.88	8.02	48.18	4.39	100
Fukuoka	4.32	9.92	5.77	9.23	5.40	**62.76**	2.61	100

(continued)

Table 25 (continued)

Pref.	x = 5th (%)	x = 10th (%)	x = 15th (%)	x = 20th (%)	x = 25th (%)	x = 31st (%)	Others (%)	Total (%)
Saga	2.91	7.94	6.33	12.09	7.21	**60.15**	3.38	100
Nagasaki	3.26	9.58	5.45	8.92	5.83	**65.02**	1.93	100
Kumamoto	3.75	9.36	5.97	9.50	4.45	**64.60**	2.37	100
Oita	2.48	9.60	5.15	9.79	6.45	**63.42**	3.11	100
Miyazaki	2.54	8.80	5.22	10.25	5.82	**63.50**	3.87	100
Kagoshima	1.96	7.36	4.60	9.97	5.87	**68.60**	1.64	100
Okinawa	3.01	5.92	3.01	2.76	3.44	**79.66**	2.20	100

Table 26 Payment day's date (=x) by industry

Industry	x = 5th (%)	x = 10th (%)	x = 15th (%)	x = 20th (%)	x = 25th (%)	x = 31st (%)	Others (%)	Total (%)
Agriculture	2.93	7.75	4.14	7.07	3.16	**73.59**	1.37	100
Forestry and hunting	0.88	5.26	5.26	8.77	8.77	**70.18**	0.88	100
Fishery	2.42	11.21	2.12	4.85	1.82	**76.36**	1.21	100
Mining	4.19	8.98	3.79	**12.97**	**15.57**	50.50	4.00	100
Construction	5.59	**14.81**	9.05	**14.84**	7.48	45.50	2.74	100
Manufacturing	6.23	**14.04**	8.84	**15.57**	7.28	45.29	2.74	100
Wholesale	4.16	**15.27**	9.34	**13.95**	4.66	50.41	2.22	100
Retail and restaurant	2.48	**13.63**	7.62	**13.47**	4.06	56.93	1.81	100
Real estate	3.30	**14.77**	5.23	8.55	4.90	**61.43**	1.81	100
Transport. and telecom.	4.51	10.67	6.03	9.86	5.58	**61.10**	2.27	100
Electr., gas, water, and heat sup.	2.29	10.86	6.29	9.71	5.14	**62.29**	3.42	100
Services	3.55	11.86	6.13	8.58	4.23	**64.06**	1.59	100

To grasp the length of the credit period in such a case, the TDB data provide us with information about the length of a credit period from the day of delivery to the day the seller actually receives cash. This information is available for the payment by promissory bills as well as by cash. Below we label these lengths (days) as LENGTH_BILLS (for payment by bills) and LENGTH_CASH (for payment by cash). As explained above, depending on when in a month a deal is done, the credit period varies by 30 days at maximum. The LENGTH_BILLS and LENGTH_CASH measure the length of the shortest credit period (i.e., the period when a deal is done on the closing day). By definition LENGTH_CASH should be equal to CP_DIFFERENCE. However, we will find some differences below. These differences might be due to the inconsistency in the methods of the TDB's research.

Before reporting our findings, it is worthwhile to note that these variables are based on the TDB's research on the firms' *ordinary* payment. In practice, firms might make payments before and after the payment is due, and so the length of the *actual* (or ex post) payment period might turn out to be different. In other words, these variables provide information about a term (length) of trade credit at the time of their contracting, or a contract term.

The TDB data show that the mean and the median duration between a closing day and a payment day is, respectively, 30.92 and 31 days for the primary payment method and 34.98 and 31 days for the secondary method (Table 27). These finding mean that a payment day usually comes one month after a closing day. Although the mean and the median are comparable in the case of the primary payment method; they are different, and the mean is longer, in the case of the secondary method. This difference means that firms can obtain more (longer) credit when they use the secondary method of payment.

Table 28 shows the frequency distribution of the difference between closing and payment days. As shown in this table, 31 days (=1 month) is the most common length, although shorter or longer durations are also observed. A negative length indicates prepayment, although it is rarely used.

Turning to LENGTH_CASH and LENGTH_BILLS (Table 29), the former is on average one month (28.15 days in mean and 30 days in median: N = 357,015). This is consistent with the results for CP_DIFFERENCE, but they are not exactly the same. The maximum length is 710 days, or about 24 months, which is extraordinarily long. It would be interesting to investigate for what characteristics of firms such a long period is allowed (or enforced). As noted above, CP_DIFFERENCE and LENGTH_CASH should by definition take the same value for each firm, but we find some differences.

Table 27 Difference between closing and payment days

	N	Mean	SD	Min	p1	p50	p99	Max
CP_DIFFERENCE for primary payment method	336,181	30.918	11.480	−31	10	31	62	187
CP_DIFFERENCE for secondary payment method	46,097	34.975	17.751	−26	5	31	93	186

Table 28 Difference between closing and payment days (frequency)

CP_DIFFERENCE for primary payment method			CP_DIFFERENCE for secondary payment method		
Days	Freq.	Percentage	Days	Freq.	Percentage
−31 to −4	111	0.03	−26 to −1	32	0.07
0	848	0.25	0	277	0.60
1–11	15,952	4.75	1–11	3,237	7.02
12–21	54,304	16.15	12–21	8,034	17.43
22–30.5	28,994	8.62	22–30	3,461	7.51
31	163,036	48.50	31	13,579	29.46
32–41	28,008	8.33	32–41	4,214	9.14
42–62	41,752	12.42	42–62	11,691	25.36
63–93	3,016	0.90	63–93	1,449	3.14
94–187	160	0.05	98–186	123	0.27
Total	336,181	100	Total	46,097	100

Table 29 Length of credit period

	N	Mean	SD	Min	p1	p50	p99	Max
LENGTH_CASH	357,015	28.146	12.521	0	1	30	60	710
LENGTH_BILLS	79,729	87.662	22.977	0	30	90	130	990

In contrast, LENGTH_BILLS is three months on average. This duration means that the sellers usually receive promissory bills of which the maturity is two months because the difference between a closing day and a payment day is usually one month. Again, the maximum of 990 days, or 33 months, is very long. It might be interesting to examine in what case such a long period is used. We should also note that the minimum of LENGTH_CASH and LENGTH_BILLS are both zero, which might be outliers. Such firms might need to be eliminated from the analysis because a promissory bill is used to make payment after the payment day. The reason for this zero payment period might be that checks (which are included in "cash") are misidentified as promissory bills by firms and/or by the TDB researchers.

3.6.2 Univariate Analysis of Payment Period (Contracted Term)

In this section, we perform the univariate analyses on the three payment period variables, CP_DIFFERENCE, LENGTH_CASH, and LENGTH_BILLS.

We first decompose the length of the credit period by industry. Beginning with CP_DIFFERENCE for the primary method of payment, its median is 31 days (1 month) for all industries (panel (1) of Fig. 30: N = 335,786). The means have

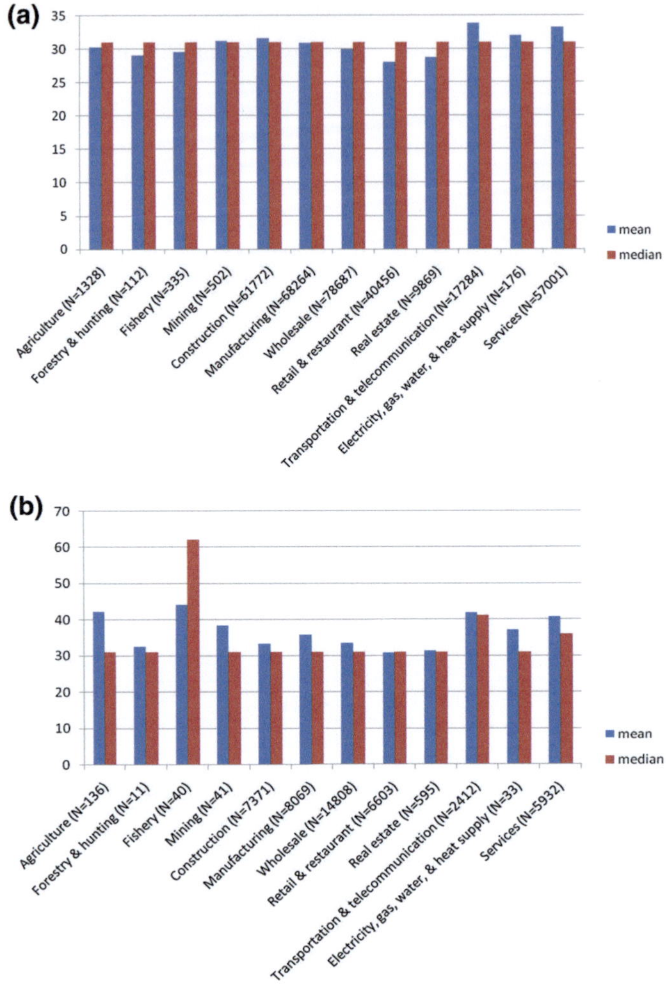

Fig. 30 Difference between closing and payment days (in days) by industry. **a** For the primary method of payment. **b** For the secondary method of payment

some variation from the shortest length (28.0 days) for Retail & restaurant to the longest length for Transportation and telecommunication (33.8 days).

As for the secondary method of payment, we see wider variations [(panel (2) of Fig. 30: N = 46,051)]. The medians for Fishery (62 days), Transportation and telecommunication (41 days), and for Services (36 days) are longer than 31 days, and the means range from 30.8 days (Retail and restaurant) to 44.1 days (Fishery). However, the number of observations for some industries, especially in the case of the secondary method of payment, is small.

The median of LENGTH_CASH is 30 days for all industries (N = 356,567) (see Fig. 31). The means differ in a similar manner to those of CP_DIFFERENCE, but

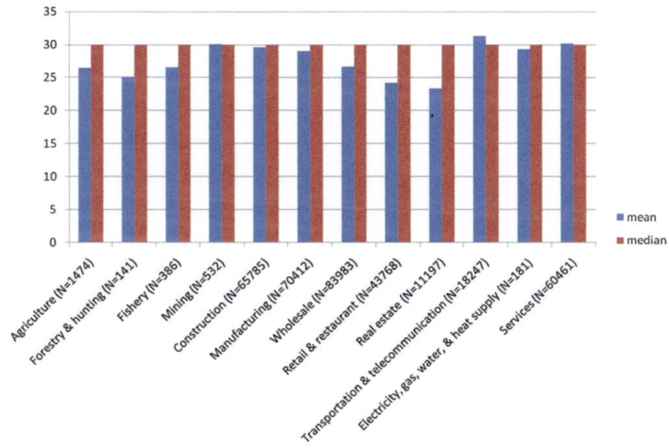

Fig. 31 Shortest credit period for cash payment (in days) by industry

their levels are shorter and their variation is slightly wider than those of CP_DIFFERENCE. The largest mean is 31.4 days for Transportation and telecommunication, which is not very long, but the shortest length of 23.4 days for Real estate is relatively short. In Sect. 3.3.1, we show that Real-estate firms depend on cash as a method of payment, but a shorter length in this figure means that the cash is paid in a relatively short period of time. This period implies that there are some real-estate firms that make immediate payments of cash. Taken together, we can conclude that trade credit is not extensively used by Real-estate firms.

Figure 32 shows the mean and median LENGTH_BILLS (N = 79,652) by industry. We can see that the median length is three months for all of the industries

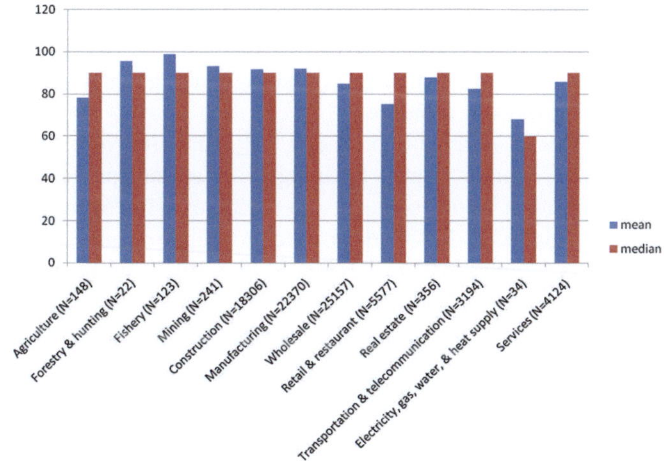

Fig. 32 Shortest credit period for promissory bill payment (in days) by industry

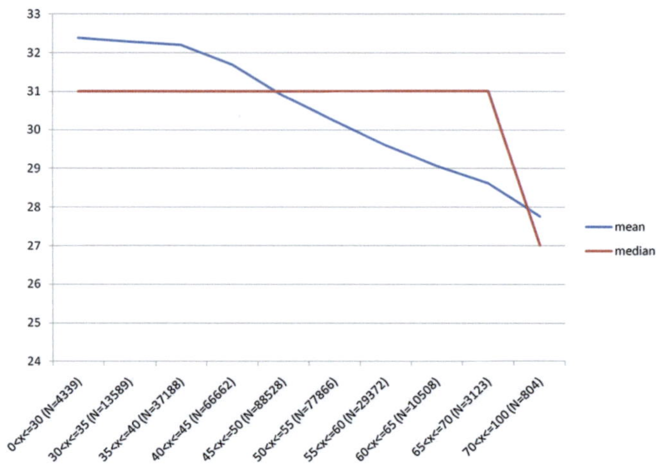

Fig. 33 Difference between closing and payment days (in days) by credit score (=x)

except for Electricity, gas, water, and heat supply (60 days). The mean length ranges from 68.0 days for Electricity, gas, water, and heat supply firms to 99.0 days for Fishery firms.

Figure 33 (N = 331,979) shows the mean and the median of CP_DIFFERENCE for the primary method of payment for different categories of credit scores. We find that the median is always 31 days, except for very creditworthy firms: the median is 27 days for firms with a credit score of 70–100. If we focus on the means, the figure more clearly shows that the credit period is shorter for more creditworthy firms (from 33.4 days for firms with a score of 0–30 to 27.8 days for firms with a score of 70–100). Also, the mean decreases with the capital asset ratio (N = 217,072: from 32.5 days for negative ratio firms to 27.7 days for firms with the ratio of 0.9–1). These findings suggest that firms with especially high repayment ability borrow short. We are not exactly sure what drives this relationship, but these super creditworthy firms might have no difficulty in making early payments, or they might have multiple closing days in a month.

As for the other base variables, the mean CP_DIFFERENCE for the primary method of payment exhibits some meaningful relationships (e.g., increasing, decreasing, U-shaped, etc.) with some of the variables. However, the mean only fluctuates within a range of 30–33 days, and no economically significant relationship exists (the number of observations are: the number of employees (N = 332,516), capital stock (N = 215,736), net current profit (N = 158,695), operating revenue (N = 151,408), the interest bearing debt to operating revenue ratio (N = 132,881), and the number of suppliers (N = 302,825)).

When we focus on CP_DIFFERENCE for the secondary method of payment, the median CP_DIFFERENCE is again almost always 31 days when interacted with the base variables. The only exception is the 62 days for firms with zero capital stock, but there are only five such firms (out of N = 31,707). The mean CP_DIFFERENCE fluctuates to a greater extent than the mean for the primary method that depends on the level of the base variables: around the range of 30–39 days. The mean length generally decreases with the number of employees (N = 45,738), credit score (N = 45,712), capital asset ratio (N = 31,874) and the number of suppliers (N = 43,413); and generally exhibits a U-shape with respect to the capital stock (N = 31,707), net current profit (N = 23,720), operating revenue (N = 22,444), and the interest bearing debt to operating revenue ratio (N = 20,196). In particular, the mean is longer for firms with more employees, a lower credit score, a smaller capital asset ratio, a large capital stock; for those recording large losses or large surpluses in terms of the net current profit, a smaller operating revenue of which the interest bearing debt to operating revenue ratio is high, and for those transacting with smaller number of suppliers.

The median of LENGTH_CASH, when categorized by the base variables, is almost always 30 days, which is consistent with the 31 day median of CP_DIFFERENCE. One exception is a shorter period for firms with a very good credit score (see Fig. 34); the median length is 28 days for firms with a score of 65–70 and 25 days for those with a score over 70 (N = 352,360). This exception suggests that firms with more repayment ability borrow short, which is consistent with the similar finding for CP_DIFFERENCE. The other exception is a shorter period (26 days) for firms that transact with more than 600 suppliers (N = 317,217).

Figure 34 also shows that the mean of LENGTH_CASH exhibits a decreasing relationship with the credit score (N = 352,360), except for firms with a very low score for which the relationship increases. The decreasing relationships are also found with respect to the number of suppliers (N = 317,217), and the capital asset ratio (from 29.8 days for firms with a negative capital asset ratio to 25.6 days for the ratio 0.9–1:N = 228,159). However, the mean generally increases with the number

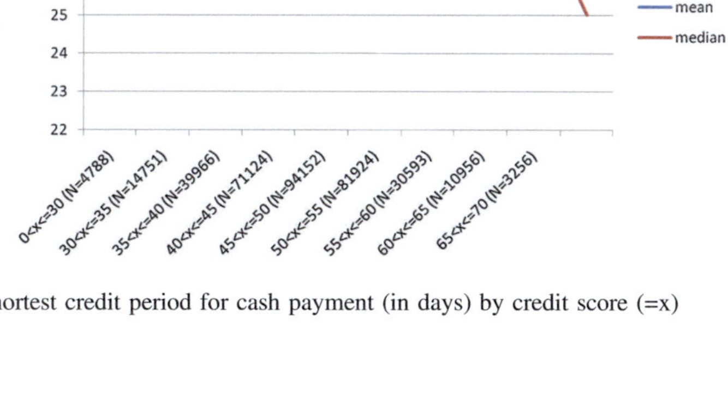

Fig. 34 Shortest credit period for cash payment (in days) by credit score (=x)

of employees (from 26.7 days for firms with no employees to 29.4 days for those with 100–300: N = 352,777), is U-shaped with respect to the capital stock (between 28.3 days and 31.2 days: N = 226,706), and is an inverted U-shape with respect to the operating revenue (between 27.4 days and 29.5 days: N = 158,791) and the interest bearing debt to operating revenue ratio (between 27.5 days and 29.4 days: N = 139,093). No clear relationship exists with respect to the net current profit (the mean ranging between 27.6 days and 28.6 days: N = 166,628), so we find no relationship between the firm performance and the credit period. As mentioned earlier, LENGTH_CASH and CP_DIFFERENCE should be equivalent by definition; thus, the differences in these univariate results are puzzling.

The median of LENGTH_BILLS is 90 days for any categories broken down by the base variables. The mean is an inverted U-shape with respect to the number of employees (ranging between 85.0 days and 88.7 days: N = 79,431), credit score (between 84.5 days and 88.2 days: N = 79,315), capital asset ratio (between 87.5 days and 89.6 days: N = 59,320), operating revenue (between 86.0 days and 90.5 days: N = 44,933), and the number of suppliers (between 82.9 days and 88.2 days: N = 76,256). The mean increases with the capital stock (between 85.8 days and 89.6 days: N = 59,100) and is V-shaped with respect to the net current profit (between 90.3 days and 97.2 days: N = 46,921). The means for the categories broken down by the interest bearing debt to operating revenue ratio range between 89.0 and 91.1 days.

3.6.3 Length of Credit Period (Actual Term)

The three variables introduced above, that is, CP_DIFFERENCE, LENGTH_CASH, and LENGTH_BILLS, measure the length of the payment period that the sample firms usually use. However, these are the lengths of the payment periods on a *contract* basis (or ex ante length). They are not necessarily the same as the actual length of a payment period (ex post length), because firms might not necessarily make payment as contracted, (i.e., at the end of the agreed payment period).[15]

One measure of the actual length of a payment period is the days in payables or in receivables. *Days in trade payables* (also known as days purchase outstanding, days payable outstanding (DPO), days payable, or days in payable) is defined as follows:

$$\text{DTP} = (\text{trade payables})/(\text{cost of goods sold}/365)$$

where trade payables are the sum of the accounts and bills payable. The days in trade payables equals 365 times the *trade debt turnover* (= trade payables/cost of

[15] Note that in the case of promissory bills, buyers rarely pay *after* the period end due to the special repayment enforcement mechanism attached to promissory bills. The same penalty is not applied to default on accounts payable (bank transfer), but anecdotal evidence shows that it also seems to be rare to make payment after its period for fear of establishing a bad reputation.

Table 30 Days in payables and receivables

	N	Mean	SD	Min	p50	Max
DTP	176,994	42.278	67.275	0	27.216	2,017.571
DTR	181,713	38.579	46.728	0	27.347	728.369

goods sold), and measures the number of days that the firms need to make repayments for their purchases.

We can also calculate a corresponding length of the period using receivables. *Days in trade receivables* (also known as days sales outstanding, days receivable, or days in receivable) is defined as follows:

$$\text{DTR} = (\text{trade receivables})/(\text{sales}/365)$$

where trade receivables are the sum of the accounts and bills receivable. The days in trade receivables is equivalent to 365 times the *trade credit turnover* (=trade payables/sales), and measures how many days the sales credit exists for. It might be interesting to calculate these days separately for cash payments and for payments by promissory bills, but it is impossible to do so because the corresponding denominators are not available.

The descriptive statistics for days in trade payables and days in trade receivables are shown in Table 30. We find that the actual lengths of the periods for making and receiving payments are both 27 days in the median. They are somewhat shorter than, but are comparable to, the mean and the median of LENGTH_CASH. However, the means are longer than the medians, especially for payments. This is probably due to the fact that the amount of promissory bills is included in the numerators. However, we can at least conclude that the actual length of the payment period is not extraordinarily different from the contracted length. We also find that the number of observations in this analysis is smaller than those for contract-based periods (used in Sect. 3.6.1). This is because the information source of these variables, that is, the financial statement information, is not available for many firms.

3.6.4 Univariate Analysis of Credit Period (Actual Term)

Similar to the variables for the contracted terms of the credit period, we can also conduct a univariate analysis on the variables that measure the actual length of the credit period. In this section, we report the results for such analyses.

Figures 35 and 36 show, the actual lengths of the periods for making and receiving payments (DTP (N = 156,500) and DTR (N = 159,699)) broken down by industry. Among the industries with many observations, the length of the period for making payments is long for Wholesale (49.6 days in median) and Manufacturing

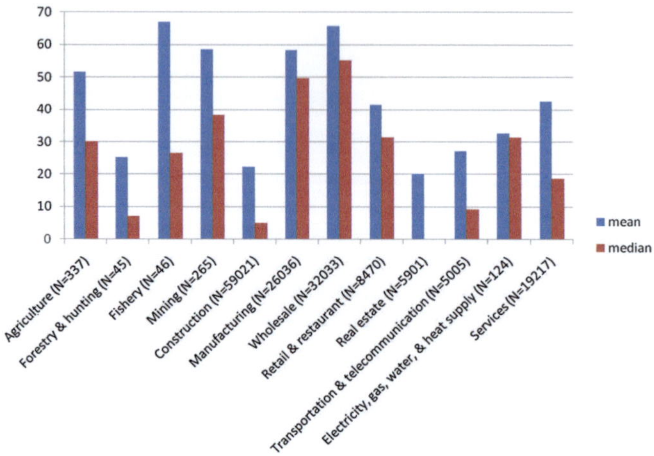

Fig. 35 Days in trade payables (in days) by industry

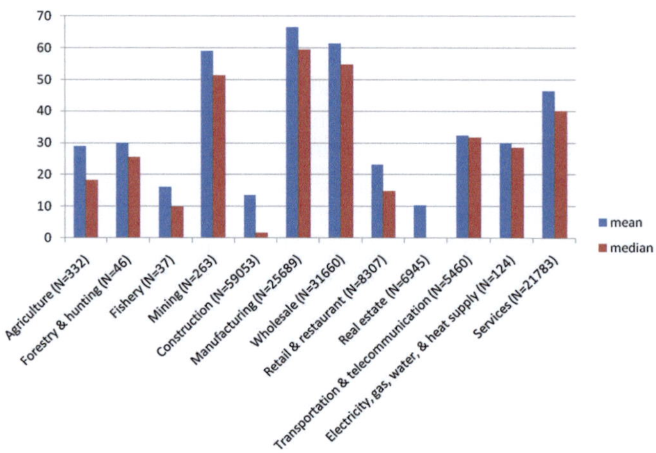

Fig. 36 Days in trade receivables (in days) by industry

(55.2 days in median), and the length of the period for receiving payments is long for Manufacturing (59.6 days in median), Wholesale (54.8 days in median), and Services (40.1 days in median). The long period for making and/or receiving payments for these industries might reflect the use of promissory bills because, as shown earlier, even the shortest credit period for a promissory bill payment (on a contract basis) is very long. This interpretation is consistent with earlier findings that the bill ratios for making and receiving payments are both high for

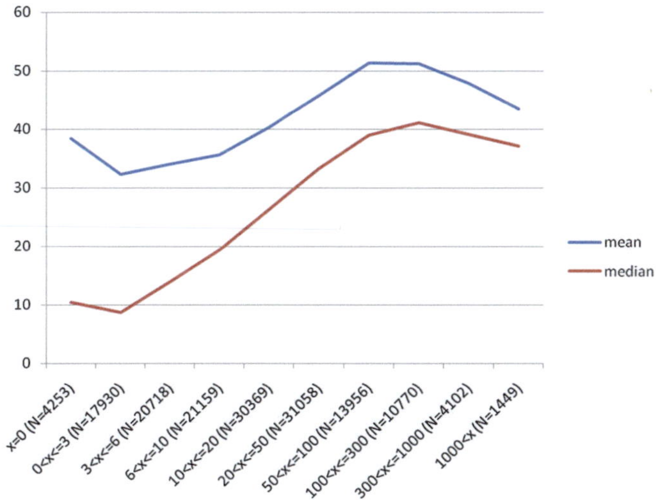

Fig. 37 Days in trade payables (in days) by firm size (x = # of employees)

Manufacturing and Wholesale firms (Sects. 3.3.3 and 3.4.3). However, another earlier finding was that Services firms do not extensively use promissory bills for receiving payments (Sect. 3.4.3), so the long payment period for receiving payments for Services firms in Fig. 36 is puzzling. This finding might rather imply that for Services firms the length of an actual payment period is longer than that of a contract-based period.

When interacted with the base variables, we find that the actual length of the periods for making and receiving payments exhibits greater variations than the contracted length of the payment period and that the variations are greater not only with respect to their means but also to their medians. Also interesting, the relationships between DTP and the base variables and those between DTR and the base variables are very similar.

For example, Fig. 37 (N = 155,764) shows that, both in means and in medians, DTP exhibits an increasing relationship with the number of employees, although they have some decreasing parts at both ends. A similar relationship also exists when DTR is interacted with the number of employees (N = 158,895).

We also find, as shown in Fig. 38 (N = 155,952), that DTP generally increases with the firms' creditworthiness. The same holds for DTR as well (N = 159,094). These findings are in contrast with our earlier finding that on a contracted basis, the length of the payment period is shorter for very creditworthy firms. Furthermore, both DTP and DTR increase with the capital stock and the operating revenue, decrease with the capital asset ratio, and are U-shaped with respect to the net current profit. Finally, DTP and DTR increase with each other. These findings suggest that further investigation into the difference between the contracted and the actual length of the credit period might be interesting.

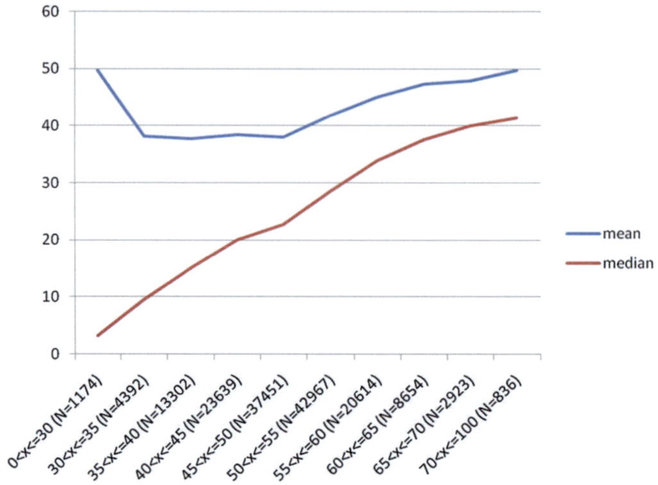

Fig. 38 Days in trade payables (in days) by credit score (=x)

3.7 Trade Credit Volume

3.7.1 Descriptive Statistics for Trade Credit Volume

In this section, we present the statistics for trade credit volume. The information on trade credit volume is available from financial statements, so the number of sample firms significantly decreases from the original (which is about 380,000).

In the means, our sample firms have 228 million yen of outstanding accounts payable and 96.6 million yen of outstanding bills payable that account for, respectively, 8.1 and 5.8 % of the total assets (Table 31). The total amount of these payables (=trade payables) is 339 million yen in the mean, and account for 13.5 % of the total assets. Because of an upward bias, their medians are smaller at 6.4 million yen (2.3 %) for accounts payable, zero for bills payable, and 22.9 million yen (7.4 %) for trade payables. The zero median for bills payable is consistent with the statistics above, which show that more than half of the firms do not use promissory bills for payments (Sect. 3.3.3).

When we count the number of the firms that do not use trade credit (i.e., zero amount), the fraction of such firms are not negligible. The firms with zero accounts payable account for 39.5 % (76,261 out of 193,327 firms), and those with zero bills payable account for 54.1 % (100,336 out of 185,575 firms). However, firms with zero trade payables account for 25.5 % (47,005 out of 184,678 firms), so there are many firms that only have a non-zero amount of accounts payable only or a non-zero amount of bills payable only.

We can also examine the statistics for the amount of receivables. As shown in Table 32, the mean accounts receivable are 351 million yen (14 % of total assets), the mean bills receivable are 68 million yen (3.5 %), and the mean trade receivables

Table 31 Volume of trade credit: payables

		N	Mean	SD	Min	Median	Max
(1) Accounts payable	Amount (thousand yen)	193,327	228,000	1,540,000	0	6,425	46,100,000
	Percentage in total asset		8.12 %	13.26 %	0.00 %	2.31 %	102.56 %
(2) Bills payable	Amount (thousand yen)	185,575	96,600	401,000	0	0	8,750,000
	Percentage in total asset		5.75 %	10.07 %	0.00 %	0.00 %	71.11 %
(3) Trade payables (=(1) + (2))	Amount (thousand yen)	184,678	339,000	1,840,000	0	22,900	49,900,000
	Percentage in total asset		13.50 %	16.82 %	0.00 %	7.38 %	111.98 %

Table 32 Volume of trade credit: receivables

		N	Mean	SD	Min	Median	Max
(1) Accounts receivable	Amount (thousand yen)	195,162	351,000	2,200,000	0	187,000	65,500,000
	Percentage in total asset		14.02 %	16.98 %	0.00 %	8.38 %	90.73 %
(2) Bills receivable	Amount (thousand yen)	185,804	68,000	331,000	0	950	7,860,000
	Percentage in total asset		3.50 %	6.56 %	0.00 %	0.26 %	52.22 %
(3) Trade receivables (=(1) + (2))	Amount (thousand yen)	185,398	438,000	2,520,000	0	30,200	71,600,000
	Percentage in total asset		17.12 %	18.60 %	0.00 %	11.49 %	92.27 %

are 138 million yen (17.12 %). Their medians are, respectively, 187 million yen (8.4 %), 950 thousand yen (0.3 %), and 30.2 million yen (11.5 %). We also find that 34.7 % of the firms (67,636 out of 195,162 firms) have zero outstanding accounts receivable, 44.2 % of the firms (82,104 out of 185,804 firms) have zero outstanding bills receivable, and 19.9 % of the firms (36,866 out of 185,398 firms) have zero outstanding trade receivables.

On balance, we find that, both in terms of means and medians, the amount of account and trade receivables are, respectively, larger than that of account and trade payables. Also, the amount of median bills receivable is larger than that of median bills payable. These findings suggest that the firms in these tables grant credit more than they receive it. As mentioned earlier, the number of observations in these tables is smaller than the original 380,000 firms because the firms in these tables are those for which financial statement information is available. Therefore, these firms are relatively transparent firms. Our findings here might thus imply that transparent firms have “deep pockets,” or can afford to provide credit to their customers.

However, the amount of mean bills receivable is smaller than that of mean bills payable; therefore, these firms receive bills less than they make them out.

3.7.2 Univariate Analysis of Trade Credit Volume

Is the amount of trade credit different depending on the firm characteristics? We now report the univariate results for trade credit volume. Note that in this analysis, we focus on the ratio of trade credit volume to total asset. That is, the results below are not for the absolute volume of trade credit. This is because the absolute volume is highly correlated with firm size, so a univariate analysis is significantly influenced by the size effect.

First, Figs. 39 and 40 show the amount of trade credit by industry. Figure 39 shows the mean and median payables to total assets ratio (accounts payable in Panel (1) and trade payables in Panel (2)). Figure 40 shows the corresponding means and medians for receivables. As these figures show, we find that trade credit is most extensively used by Wholesale firms. For example, for wholesale firms, the trade payables to the total asset ratio is on average 27.7 % (in the mean) or 24.0 % (in the median), and trade receivables account for 32.0 % (in the mean) or 30.1 % (in the median) of their total assets. The trade credit is also somewhat extensively used by Manufacturing and Retail and restaurant firms for making payments, and by Manufacturing, Services, and Transportation and telecommunication firms for receiving payments. Consistent with the results in earlier sections, Real-estate firms rarely use trade credit both for making and receiving payments.

Figures 41 and 42 show the results when we focus on promissory bills. If we focus on industries with large observations, promissory bills are extensively used by Wholesale and Manufacturing firms, and to a lesser extent by Construction firms. Mining firms also use promissory bills, but their number of observations is small. These findings are generally consistent with our finding earlier with respect to the ratios of the methods to make and receive payments. However, if we focus on the medians, the firms in many industries do not use promissory bills either for making or receiving payments.

When we interact trade credit volume with the base variables, we first find that the results for accounts payable are very similar to those for trade payables. The results for accounts receivable are also similar to those for trade receivables. These are probably because the amount of promissory bills is relatively small (see Tables 31 and 32). Second, we also find that the results for trade payables and those for trade receivables are similar as well. We report the results for trade payables as representative results, and do not report other results unless we find a significant difference. Finally, regarding promissory bills, we find that univariate results on the bills payable and those on bills receivable are different from those on trade payables and trade receivables, and they are also slightly different from each other. So we present the results on bills payable, and report those on bills receivable if notable differences exist.

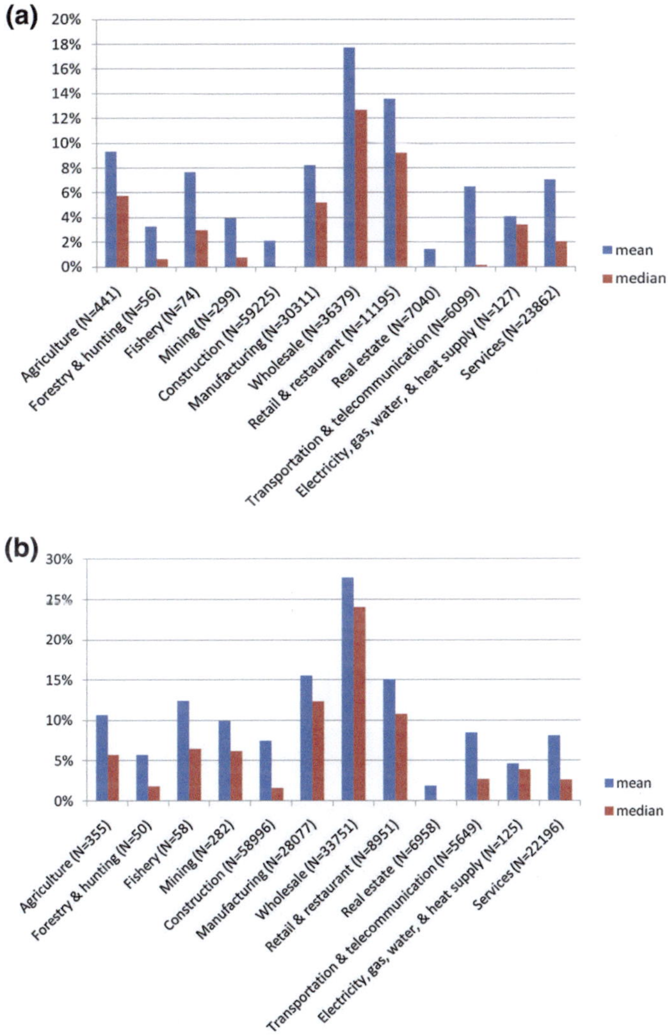

Fig. 39 Payables to total assets ratio by industry. **a** Accounts payable to total assets (N = 175,108). **b** Trade payables to total assets (N = 165,448)

As Fig. 43 shows (N = 164,630), trade payables generally increases with the number of employees, although they decrease when the number is very large. A similar relationship appears with respect to trade receivables (N = 165,474), accounts payable (N = 174,199), and accounts receivable (N = 176,201). However, their means, and to a lesser extent their medians as well, decrease when the number of employees is very small. That is, they exhibit a rotated-S shape. Furthermore, in the case of mean accounts payable, the decrease for the largest firms does not exist; therefore, the mean exhibits a U-shape. However, on balance larger firms have

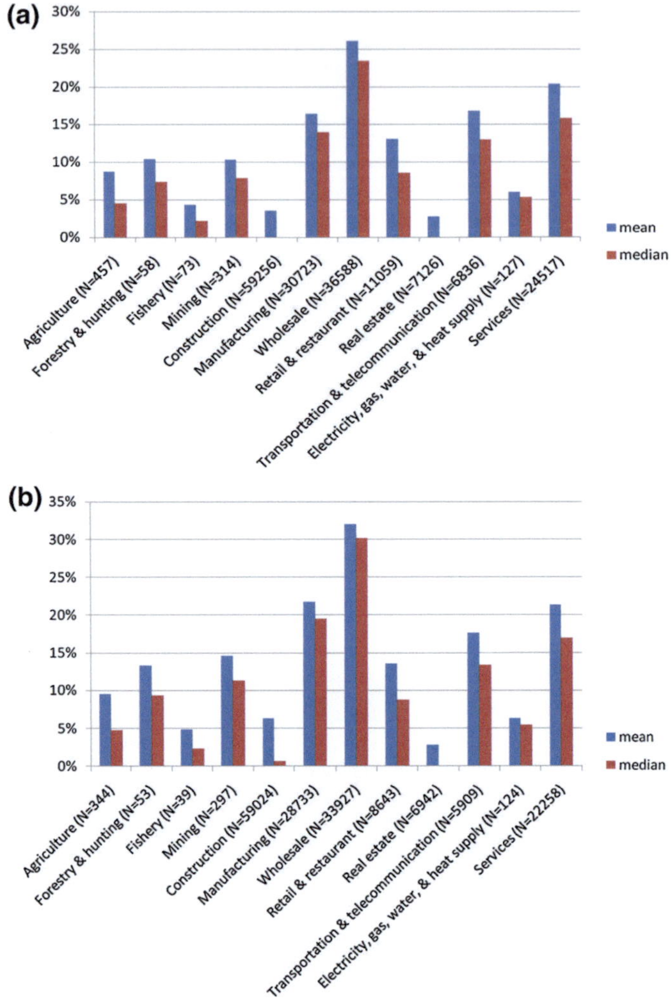

Fig. 40 Receivables to total assets ratio by industry. **a** Accounts receivable to total assets (N = 177,134). **b** Trade receivables to total assets (N = 166,293)

larger amounts of trade credit, and smaller firms have smaller amounts. Similar characteristics also appear when these amounts are interacted with the credit score; on balance more creditworthy firms have larger amounts of trade credit, and less creditworthy firms have smaller amounts.

We also find that trade payables, trade receivables, accounts payable, and accounts receivable generally decreases with the capital asset ratio (N = 178,464, 179,257, 187,904, and 189,879, respectively) and with the interest bearing debt to operating revenue ratio (N = 161,285, 161,194, 160,575, and 160,430, respectively); and generally increase with capital stock (N = 178,492, 179,298, 187,773,

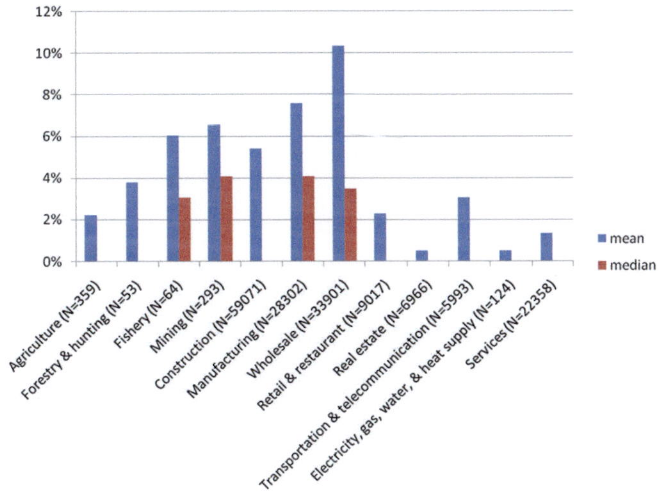

Fig. 41 Bills payable to total assets by industry (N = 166,501)

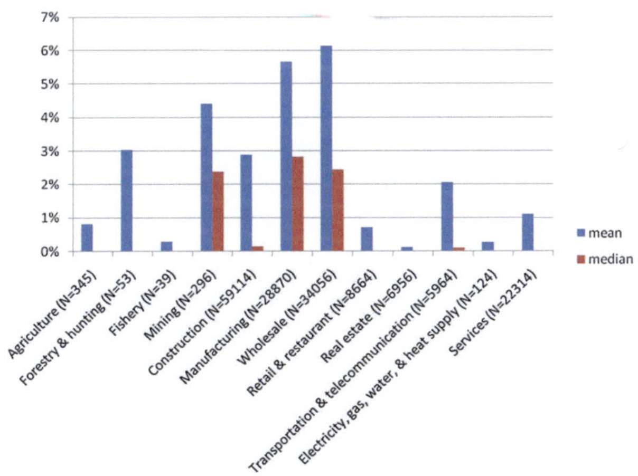

Fig. 42 Bills receivable to total assets by industry (N = 166,795)

and 189,715, respectively) and the operating revenue (N = 178,495, 178,532, 178,886, and 178,953, respectively). They are V- or U-shaped with respect to the net current profit (N = 179,248, 179,447, 181,627, and 182,038, respectively). The findings here are almost similar to the findings for the actual length of the trade credit (i.e., DTP and DTR reported in Sect. 3.6.4). This similarity implies that the volume of credit and the length of the credit period are correlated.

Both the bills payable (Fig. 44: N = 165,860) and the bills receivable (N = 165,975) exhibit an inverted U-shape with respect to the number of employees. We find that firms hiring 50–100 employees use promissory bills the

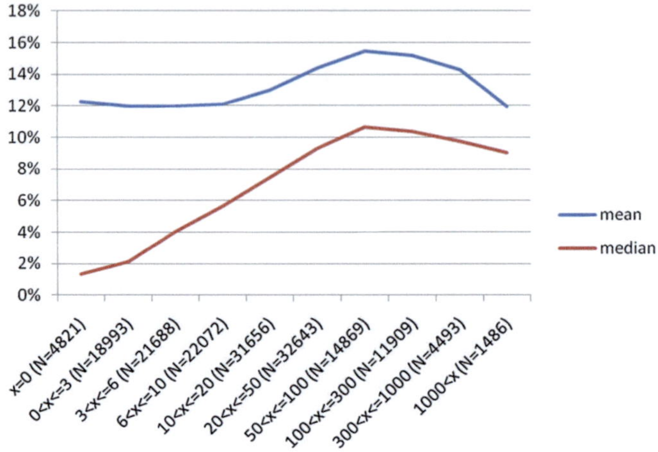

Fig. 43 Trade payables to total assets ratio by firm size (x = # of employees)

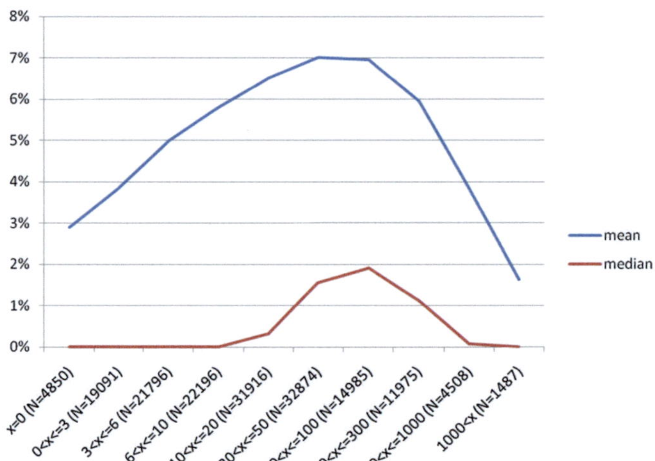

Fig. 44 Bills payable to total assets ratio by firm size (x = # of employees)

most for both making and receiving payments. A relationship of a similar shape also exists with respect to the credit score (N = 179,469 for bills payable and 166,152 for bills receivable) and to operating revenue (N = 178,507 for bills payable and 178,541 for bills receivable). We find that the firms that are scored 55–60 use the bills the most extensively. An inverted U-shape further exists with respect to the capital asset ratio (N = 179,471 for bills payable and 179,732 for bills receivable), capital stock (179,484 and 179,751), and interest bearing debt operating revenue ratio (161,171 and 161,132), although the peak is located far to the left in the case of bills payable versus the capital asset ratio, bills payable versus interest bearing debt to operating revenue ratio, and bills receivable versus interest bearing debt to operating revenue ratio. No clear relationship exists between bills payable or bills receivable and the net current profit (N = 179,461 and 179,536, respectively).

3.8 Bills Discounted

3.8.1 Descriptive Statistics for Bills Discounted

As mentioned in Sect. 3.2, promissory bills are often discounted by banks. Having banks discount promissory bills (*tegata-waribiki*) is a traditional method for short-term financing in Japan. A firm asks a bank to buy bills it has received from buyers of its products at a discounted price with recourse. When the drawer of a bill fails to make payments, the firm is obliged to make the payment for the bill. For a limited number of firms, the TDB database contains information of the amount of bills discounted.

Table 33 shows the descriptive statistics for the amount of bills discounted. The mean and median amounts of bills discounted are respectively 60 and 14 million yen. For reference, we find in Table 31 that the amount of promissory bills payable is 96.6 million yen (in mean) and zero (in median) (N = 185,575). The means indicate that about 60 % of the promissory bills are discounted by banks, although this inference is far from exact because of the difference in the numbers of observations.

Table 33 also shows the descriptive statistics for the amount of bills discounted by main banks. Main banks in the TDB database are defined by the firms as the banks that are most important to them, and the definition is subjective.[16] However, from these figures we can understand to what extent the firms rely on a specific bank. We find that the mean and median amounts of bills discounted by main banks are respectively 29 and 6 million yen. Compared with the total amount of bills discounted, we find that a sizable fraction of the discounting was made by firms' main banks.

The third row of Table 33 shows the concentration ratio of the bills discounted to the main banks. The concentration ratio is defined as the amount of bills discounted by the main banks to the total amount of bills discounted.[17] The mean concentration ratio is 57.5 % but the median is 90.8 %. This finding means that more than half of the sample firms rely almost solely on their main banks as discounters. When we

[16] For more on the definition of a main bank in the TDB database, see Ono et al. (forthcoming).

[17] As explained earlier in this monograph, we eliminate observations as outliers if a variable from the financial statement takes the value that falls into the largest and the smallest 0.1 % ranges. However, with respect to this concentration ratio, we drop observations if the ratio takes the value that exceeds 100 %.

Table 33 The amount of bills discounted (thousand yen)

	N	Mean	SD	Min	p1	p50	p99	Max
Bills discounted (thousand yen)	57,423	60,000	194,000	0	0	14,000	770,000	5,000,000
Bills discounted by main banks (amount: thousand yen)	36,737	28,600	72,700	0	0	6,000	350,000	1,350,000
Bills discounted by main banks (concentration ratio: %)	36,025	57.5	46.3	0	0	90.8	100	100

examine the data more closely, we find that the distribution for the concentration ratio is highly bipolarized. The percentage of firms that have positive amounts of bills discounted but do not have their main banks discount them (i.e., firms with the concentration ratio being zero) is 35.6 %, whereas almost half (49.7 %) of the firms exclusively rely on main banks (concentration ratio is 95–100 %). We confirm that for the majority of firms, main banks are the sole discounter of their promissory bills, but a sizable fraction of firms do not rely on main banks as discounters.

3.8.2 Univariate Analysis of the Use of Bills Discounted

In our sample (N = 57,423), 26.1 % of the firms do not use bills discounted at all. We then examine whether the non-use of bills discounted is related to the firm characteristics. Regarding the firms' industry, the bills discounted is used most extensively by Manufacturing firms, with the percentage of non-users being 14.3 %. In contrast, they are rarely used in Real estate (95.3 %) and Retail and restaurant (77.0 %). When we examine the use by region, we find that the percentage of non-users is smaller in the Osaka (6.0 %) and Aichi (2.9 %) prefectures. This might be because both large and small manufacturing firms are agglomerated in these prefectures.

Figure 45 shows the fraction of firms that do not use bills discounted for different firm-size categories. We find that the fraction is U-shaped, and both small and large firms tend not to use bills discounted. A similar relationship is found with respect to the credit score as well.

3.9 Factoring

Finally, we provide some information on the use of *factoring*. Factoring is a transaction where a lender called a *factor* purchases the accounts receivable of firms. It is therefore a form of discounting. However, factors can purchase multiple

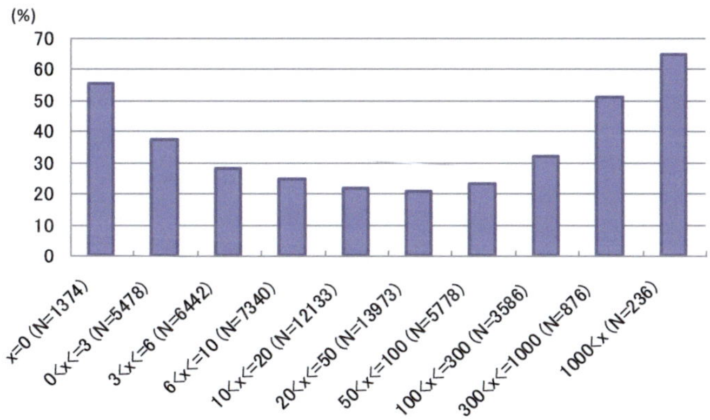

Fig. 45 Percentages of firms with no outstanding for bills discounted by firm size (x = # of employees)

Table 34 Usage of factoring

	Freq.	Percentage
Not used	165,980	44.88
Used	29,053	7.85
Unknown	174,836	47.27
Total	369,869	100.00

receivables collectively and/or future receivables. Thus, factoring is essentially lending collateralized by accounts receivable. The credit is explicitly linked to the value of a borrower's underlying assets and not to the borrower's overall creditworthiness.[18] However, factors only purchase accounts receivable and do not purchase promissory bills (bills receivable).

The TDB data show that about 7.9 % of the sample firms use factoring (Table 34). However, note that we have an independent category, unknown, that indicates that the use/non-use of factoring is not identified. Excluding those firms, 14.9 % of the firms use factoring.

When we divide sample firms depending on their industry, even if we include the "unknown" firms (N = 369,520: Fig. 46), factoring is extensively used by Manufacturing firms (18.8 %). Factoring is also used by Wholesale (9.1 %), Mining (7.5 %), Construction (6.7 %), Transportation and telecommunication (4.6 %), and Service (3.3 %) firms. Less than 1 % of the firms in other industries use factoring.

As Fig. 47 shows, the fraction of firms using factoring (including the "unknown" firms) exhibits an inverted-U shape with respect to firm size (N = 364,856).

[18] For more on factoring, see Bakker et al. (2004).

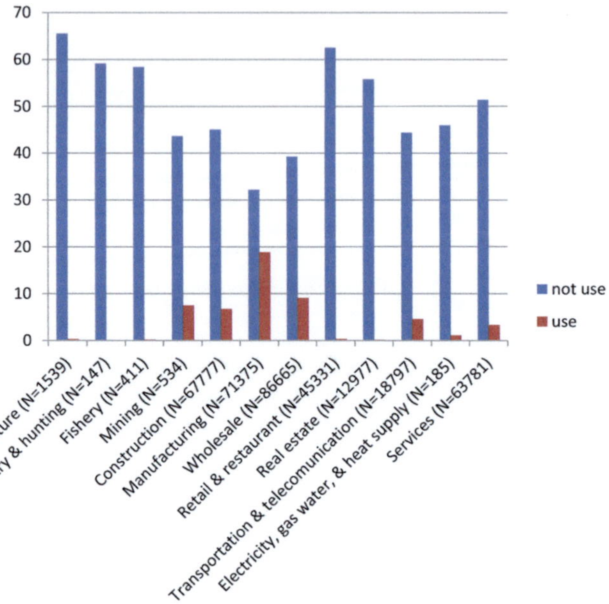

Fig. 46 The fraction of firms using factoring (%) by industry

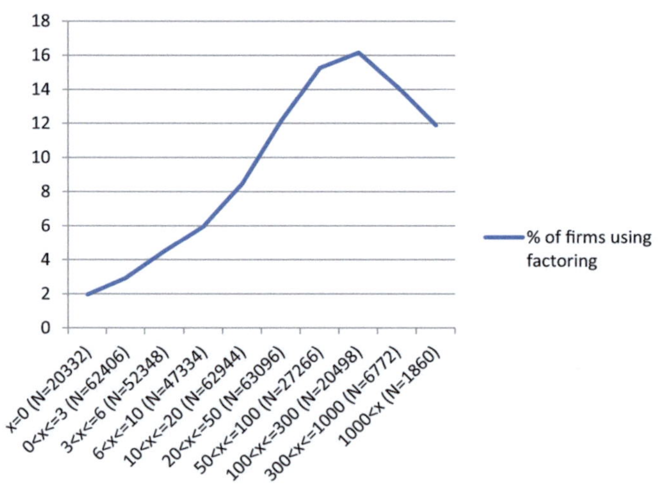

Fig. 47 The fraction of firms using factoring (%) by firm size (x = # of employees)

The firms with 100–300 employees use factoring more extensively (16.2 %). It is possible that these firms transact with large firms for which accounts receivable are highly creditworthy and easy to liquidate. An inverted-U shape also exists with respect to the credit score (firms with the score of 65–70 use factoring the most

(16.9 %, N = 364,342)), capital asset ratio (firms with the ratio 0.2–0.3 use the most (12.0 %, N = 234,416)), capital stock (firms with the stock of 50–100 million yen use the most (15.2 %, N = 232,911)), and the operating revenue (firms earning a profit of 5–10 billion yen use the most (19.8 %, N = 162,744)). The fraction of firms that use factoring exhibits a U-shape with respect to the net current profit, with the fraction larger for the firms in the lowest (17.1 %) and the highest profit categories (15.9 %, N = 170,770).

The fraction of firms that use factoring is larger for firms with more trade receivables. The fraction generally increases with the amount of accounts receivable (N = 176,173). The fraction also generally increases with CP_DIFFERENCE (the length of the period from the closing day to the payment day) for the primary method of payment, although the increase is not monotone (N = 334,821).

Is there any relation between having banks discount promissory bills and having factors discount accounts receivable? We find that the use of factoring is larger when firms use promissory bills discounted by banks more extensively. First, as Fig. 48 shows, the more the firms have their banks discount their promissory bills, the more the fraction of firms that use factoring becomes.

Factoring and bills discounting are both methods of liquidating trade credit. It might be interesting to examine different (and simultaneous) uses of bill discounting (having banks discount promissory bills) and of factoring (having factors discount accounts receivable). It is intriguing to examine whether the strong enforcement mechanism for payment attached to promissory bills only makes any differences.

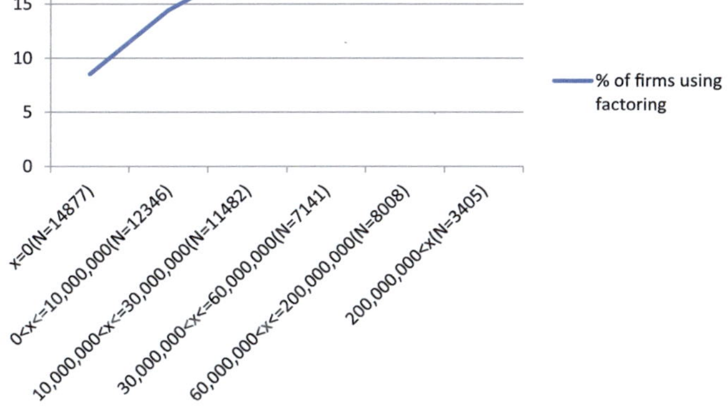

Fig. 48 The fraction of firms using factoring (%) by discounted bills (x = amount of bills discounted)

4 Legal System Relevant to Interfirm Relationships in Japan

This section provides the legal background that might be relevant when examining the interfirm relationships and trade credit in Japan. The interfirm relationship, or trade credit, has attracted less attention from legal scholars, still less from law reformers. The lack of attention might partly be because the relevant laws are scattered in various spheres of the law: in the Civil Law countries like Japan, some of the rules are contained in the law of obligations, some are in bankruptcy law, and still others are in corporate law. As far as the reservation of title to the supplied goods is concerned, some countries treat it as a kind of security interest and discuss it within the framework of secured transactions. Except for bankruptcy law, which has been one of the focuses of law reform after the Asian Financial Crisis at the end of 1990s, these subjects have not been considered the target of law reform. With relatively rich discussions on the subject in the economics literature, the lack of their influence on legal theories is interesting.

However, the issue of the interfirm relationship requires an integrated approach based on legal as well as economic theories. It is for this reason that we summarize the laws in Japan in relation to these issues in this section.

4.1 Regulation on Payment Terms by the Subcontracting Act

The most important law about trade credit in Japan is the Subcontracting Act (The Act against Delay in Payment of Subcontract Proceeds to Subcontractors). Its apparent aim is to prevent the abuse of contractual power by principal contractors (as purchasers) against small- and medium-sized subcontractors (as suppliers). The Act requires the purchaser to make payment within 60 days of the supply of goods or services when the supply agreement qualifies as "subcontracting." The case in which an agreement is considered as subcontracting is: when the purchaser commissions the supply of goods or services to the supplier, and the purchaser qualifies a size criterion and is thus considered as being large enough to abuse its power over the supplier.[19]

[19] If the agreement is for the supply of goods, the regulation applies when (i) the purchaser (principal contractor) is a corporation with the stated capital of more than 300 million yen, and the supplier (subcontractor) is an individual or a corporation with the stated capital of 300 million yen or less; or (ii) the purchaser is a corporation with the stated capital of 300 million yen or less but more than 10 million yen, and the supplier is an individual or a corporation with the stated capital of 10 million yen or less. In the case of the supply of services or information-based products (such as computer programs or movies), the regulation applies when (i) the purchaser is a corporation with the stated capital of more than 50 million yen, and the supplier is an individual or a corporation with the stated capital of 50 million yen or less; or (ii) the purchaser is a corporation

Some theories of trade credit in the field of economics predict that a two-part term for payment can be used as a device for screening creditworthy buyers (Smith 1987; Ng et al. 1999). The two-part term means that the seller gives the buyer a discount if the payment is made earlier. Such a two-part term is prohibited under the Subcontracting Act in Japan unless the effective interest rate equals the prime rate for the short-term lending.

4.2 Price Discrimination and the Antimonopoly Act

Other theories in economics regard trade credit as a tool for price discrimination (e. g., Schwartz and Whitcomb 1979; Brennan et al. 1988). If it means that large-scale buyers receive more favorable credit terms (Klapper et al. 2010), it could be regulated by the Antimonopoly Act. The Antimonopoly Act, which is the competition law in Japan, prohibits, as an unfair trade practice, the act of "unjustly" discriminating against the buyer with regards to the payment. Whether "unjust" or not is determined by the Japan Fair Trade Commission based on their analysis on the anticompetitive effects of the price discrimination, subject to the review of the court.

Another argument regarding price discrimination can be made regarding the case where trade credit is offered regardless of the creditworthiness of the buyer. From an economics standpoint, such a practice results in reducing the effective price for the low-credit buyer (Petersen and Rajan 1997; Ng et al. 1999). However, this is less likely to constitute an unfair trade practice because the trade term is nondiscriminatory on its face.

4.3 The Retention of Title

Some studies in economics consider that a supplier has a special advantage to liquidate the goods that it supplied when the buyer is in default. This advantage makes it possible for the supplier to grant more credit to the buyer than other creditors can (Longhofer and Santos 2003; Frank and Maksimovic 2005; Fabbri and Menichini 2010). Legally speaking, the general rule is that the seller as an unsecured creditor is treated equally with other creditors. Under this rule, while the supplier as a creditor can ask the court for the attachment and forced sale of any asset of the buyer when the latter defaults, other creditors can also request distribution of the proceeds from the attached asset. In this sense, the comparative

(Footnote 19 continued)
with the stated capital of 50 million yen or less but more than 10 million yen, and the supplier is an individual or a corporation with the stated capital of 10 million yen or less.

advantage of the supplier, if any, in liquidating the supplied goods does not explain the offer of trade credit by the supplier. In this sense, the supplier advantage theory has no legal grounds in Japan.

However, there are some cases in which suppliers might be able to repossess the goods they sold, and to exercise their special advantage, if any, to liquidate the goods. The supplier might retain the title to the supplied goods until the payment is made by inserting a specific clause in that contract. Such a clause for the *retention of title* is valid under Japanese law. Its private enforcement in case of default, namely the recovery of the delivered goods without asking for the court order, is also permitted unless the buyer files for the insolvency procedure and the court issues an order of stay. Even in the absence of the retention of title by the agreement, the supplier is entitled to *a lien for the purchase money on the goods supplied*. When the buyer sells the goods to a third party, the supplier is subrogated to the claim for payment by that third party. The enforcement of the lien cannot be made privately but needs a court order so the bailiff can seize the goods.

When the insolvency procedure commences, the retention of title is treated as a kind of security interest. The supplier can enforce its right notwithstanding the commencement of the procedure in the case of *bankruptcy (liquidation)*, but its right is stayed and subjected to administration by the court under the *corporate reorganization procedure*. If the commenced procedure is *civil rehabilitation (DIP procedure)*, a security interest, including the retention of title, can be enforced notwithstanding; but is subject to the stay order by the court as well as the request for extinction for consideration if some conditions are met. Thus the supplier's advantage in liquidating the goods when the buyer becomes insolvent might be limited depending on which procedure is filed for.

4.4 Protection of Creditors Under the Companies Act

Finally, another economic theory predicts that the degree to which a creditor is protected against the diversion of the asset might affect the decision of whether or not to offer trade credit (Fabbri and Menichini 2010). It might be worth noting that creditors of a joint stock company can seek damages when the manager of the company does harm to it intentionally or by gross negligence under the Japanese Companies Act. The diversion could be deterred by such a remedy to some extent.

5 Conclusion

In this monograph, we report the current status of interfirm transactions with a special emphasis on trade credit. We present descriptive statistics from a huge corporate data set for Japan and conduct univariate analyses of them. We also provide the legal background that might be relevant when conducting further analysis using this data set. As we have documented thus far, we find many intriguing characteristics of interfirm relationships in Japan. Namely, we find that:

- The use/non-use of different methods of payment differ depending on industries and regions
- The terms of payment also differ depending on industries and regions
- However, the use/non-use and the terms of trade credit depend on other firm characteristics
- Factoring is used by relatively creditworthy firms

We have provided many possible explanations for the economic mechanisms working behind these findings. However, they are after all speculations based on descriptive statistics or univariate results. Deeper analysis using more elaborate techniques, at least a multivariate analysis, needs to be conducted.

References

Bakker, M.H.R., L.F. Klapper, and G.F. Udell. 2004. *Financing small and medium-size enterprises with factoring: Global growth and its potential in Eastern Europe*. World Bank.

Bates, J., and D.L. Hally. 1982. *The Financing of small business*, 3rd ed. London: Sweet & Maxwell.

Brennan, M.J., V. Maksimovic, and J. Zechner. 1988. Vendor financing. *Journal of Finance* 43:1127–1141.

Emery, G.W., and K. Ariga. 1996. Some evidence on the trade credit practices of Japanese trading companies. *Advances in Pacific Basin Financial Markets* 2B:237–249.

Fabbri, D. and A.M.C. Menichini. 2010. Trade credit, collateral liquidation, and borrowing constraints. *Journal of Financial Economics* 96:413–432.

Frank, M.Z., and V. Maksimovic. 2005. *Trade credit, collateral, and adverse selection*. Mimeo: University of Minnesota and University of Maryland.

James, J.A., and D.F. Weiman. 2010. From drafts to checks: The evolution of correspondent banking networks and the formation of the modern U.S. payment system, 1950–1014. *Journal of Money, Credit, and Banking* 42:237–265.

Klapper, L.F, L. Laeven, and R. Rajan. 2010. Trade credit contracts. *Review of Financial Studies* 25:838–867.

Longhofer, S.D., and J.A.C. Santos. 2003. The paradox of priority. *Financial Management* 32:69–8.

Matsumura, T. and M. Ryser. 1995. Revelation of private information about unpaid notes in the trade credit bill system in Japan. *Journal of Legal Studies* 24:165–187.

Miwa, Y. and M. Ramseyer. 2008. The implications of trade credit for bank monitoring: Suggestive evidence from Japan. *Journal of Economics & Management Strategy* 17:317–343.

Ng, C.K., J.K. Smith, and R.L. Smith. 1999. Evidence on the determinants of credit terms used in interfirm trade. *Journal of Finance* 54:1109–1129.

Ono, A., H. Uchida, S. Kozuka, and M. Hazama. A new look at bank-firm relationships and the use of collateral in Japan: Evidence from Teikoku Databank Data. In *The economics of interfirm networks* (*Advances in Japanese Business and Economics*), eds. T. Watanabe, I. Uesugi, and A. Ono, Vol. 4, Chap. 12. Springer (forthcoming).

Petersen, M.A., and R. Rajan. 1997. Trade credit: Theory and evidence. *Review of Financial Studies* 10:661–691.

Schwartz, R.A. and D.K. Whitcomb. 1979. The trade credit decision. In *Handbook of financial economics*, ed. J.L. Bicksler. North Holland.

Smith, J.K. 1987. Trade credit and informational asymmetry. *Journal of Finance* 42:863–872.

Steffen, R. 1964. *Cases on commercial and investment paper*, 3rd edn. Brooklyn the Foundation Press, Inc.

Uchida, H., I. Uesugi, and M. Hotei. 2010. Repayment enforcement and informational advantages: Empirical determinants of trade credit use. RIETI discussion paper 10-E-041. The Research Institute of Economy, Trade, and Industry.

Uesugi, I., H. Uchida, Y. Ogura, A. Ono, X. Peng, D. Tsuruta, T. Nemoto, H. Hirata, Y. Yasuda, N. Yamori, W. Watanabe, and M. Hotei. 2009. Current status of SMEs under the financial crisis: Summary of the results of '*Survey on Transaction with Firms and Financial Institutions* (February 2008)' and '*Survey on Transaction with Firms and Financial Institutions under the Financial Crisis* (February 2009)'. RIETI discussion paper 09-J-020. The Research Institute of Economy, Trade, and Industry.

Index

© The Author(s) 2015
H. Uchida et al., *Interfirm Relationships and Trade Credit in Japan*,
SpringerBriefs in Economics, DOI 10.1007/978-4-431-55187-4

MIX
Papier aus verantwortungsvollen Quellen
Paper from responsible sources
FSC® C105338

If you have any concerns about our products,
you can contact us on
ProductSafety@springernature.com

In case Publisher is established outside the EU,
the EU authorized representative is:
Springer Nature Customer Service Center GmbH
Europaplatz 3, 69115 Heidelberg, Germany

Printed by Libri Plureos GmbH
in Hamburg, Germany